Progress in IS

For further volumes:
http://www.springer.com/series/10440

Gino Brunetti · Thomas Feld
Lutz Heuser · Joachim Schnitter
Christian Webel

Editors

Future Business Software

Current Trends in Business Software Development

Springer

Editors
Gino Brunetti
Software-Cluster
Darmstadt
Germany

Thomas Feld
Scheer Group GmbH
Saarbrücken
Germany

Lutz Heuser
Urban Software Institute
  GmbH & Co. KG
Walldorf
Germany

Joachim Schnitter
SAP AG
Walldorf
Germany

Christian Webel
Fraunhofer IESE
Kaiserslautern
Germany

ISSN 2196-8705   ISSN 2196-8713   (electronic)
ISBN 978-3-319-34292-4   ISBN 978-3-319-04144-5   (eBook)
DOI 10.1007/978-3-319-04144-5
Springer Cham Heidelberg New York Dordrecht London

Printed on acid-free paper

Springer is part of Springer Science+Business Media (www.springer.com)

Foreword

Business software is a key driver of innovation in today's business environment. The aim of this volume it to provide prospects toward the future business software and insights into current trends in business software development. The target audience are software developers, IT practitioners, and researchers from the domains business software, security, cloud computing, software technology, and related domains.

The volume is organized into three parts. In Part I, Fischer and Jost from SAP AG and Software AG, the two largest German software houses and international key players in the business software segment, provide their views on emerging business networks, the potential for business software behind the cloud technology, and the future of business software. Part II about emergent software introduces the characteristics of the next generation of business software. Part III about agile software development addresses new trends in software development and provides insights about respective strategies and experiences of SAP AG and Software AG.

The new paradigm of emergent software addresses the highly complex requirements of tomorrow's business software. It aims at dynamically and flexibly combining a multiplicity of components from various providers and adapting itself more easily to new market or business requirements without major efforts for software integration. A wide range of different services is increasingly offered and used in the Internet via cloud platforms in a cost-effective and efficient way (see Fig. 1). In this environment, emergent software is an approach to fulfill the highly complex requirements of digital companies, i.e., companies that have digitalized most or all of their business processes such that business software becomes the decisive driver behind product and process innovation.

Emergent software can adapt itself dynamically to the changing requirements of the market as well as the business environment and supports service relationships between companies. The intelligent linking of existing offers and the addition of supplementary components and services allows a completely new range of services to be provided.

Companies that make use of emergent software will be able to realize new business models—models that would have been unthinkable during the original development of the components and services. Users of emergent software receive individual solutions via the simple composition of standard solutions from

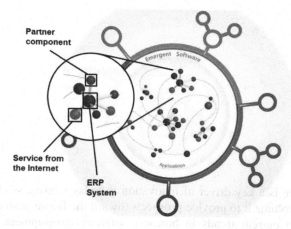

Partner
component

Service from
the Internet

ERP
System

Fig. 1 The emergent software paradigm

multiple providers. This means emergent software will be relatively easy to maintain and, furthermore, will not require significant investments for integration on user side. Users will therefore be able to increase the flexibility of their new and innovative business models, operate them in a more market-oriented manner, and map them within their software systems.

One challenge addressed by Rombach et al. from the Fraunhofer Institute for Experimental Software Engineering (IESE) is how to measure the impact of emergent software, i.e., how to determine the benefit of these methodological and technological solutions with regard to business goals. This requires a goal-oriented measurement approach encompassing the definition of measurement goals, the definition of metrics, and the interpretation of the measured data in the underlying context. Their contribution to this book outlines an approach for quantitatively evaluating the techniques and tools developed to measure the impact of emergence in business applications.

The article by Kleeberg et al. from the SEEBURGER AG analyzes current practices and upcoming trends of information systems integration in the context of cloud computing technology. Therefore, cloud integration scenarios and related challenges from multiple perspectives are discussed. Modern enterprise IT landscapes increasingly include best-of-breed business applications, platforms, and infrastructure sourced on demand from cloud service providers. Such IT cloud sourcing fosters both scalability and flexibility of enterprise information systems, which enables fast responses to ever-changing market needs and competition.

However, cloud computing also extends the need for information systems integration on the levels of data, components, and processes, also beyond the boundaries of a single enterprise. Furthermore, integration technology providers increasingly offer their solutions as-a-service in the cloud, which allows them to extend their portfolios in response to technology trends like big data or mobile outreach. Kleeberg et al. also draw a vision of a cloud-based integration technology stack that enables a wide range of federated cloud integration solutions.

Business Process Management (BPM) is the next important issue related to the emergent software systems discussed in this volume. Feld and Hoffmann from the Scheer Group argue that nowadays managers are facing a fast-moving business environment with changing customer needs and expectations, fast-evolving technologies and product lifecycles, strong globalization effects, accelerating innovation, and increasing digitization of products. Within this environment, managers need to ensure long-term business success for their company. In a growing market, it is important to respond by investing in innovative new products, sales channels, and marketing strategies.

Organizations operating in a tough economic environment also need to focus on optimizing costs, timescales, and product resources in order to boost efficiency. According to Feld and Hoffmann, long-term business success is all about the ability of an organization to respond quickly to the changing market conditions, adapting their business model, and bringing their market strategy to operational execution through appropriate business processes, people, and technologies. BPM is essential to ensure this long-term business success based on flexible, market-responsive structures that simultaneously promote efficiency. The challenge is the management of individualized process variants. The authors therefore introduce process on demand as an extended methodology for BPM and the implementation of business processes that enables a flexible and rapid adoption.

The part about emergent software as main characteristic of future business software solutions is rounded up by the aspect of IT security. Cross-company emergent business models can only be successful if they are trusted. This implies that they have an adequate level of security. Important security features include the ability to identify components and their properties to reliably verify the correct functioning of services, while protecting the privacy of individuals, organizations, and businesses properly. The properties of components and services and the protection goals for the data must be specified in order to enforce the appropriate security features at the various levels of the system.

Emergent business software is highly dynamic and flexible. Monolithic security solutions cannot secure the service composites that this new paradigm enables. Instead, different security services have to be combined in order to provide flexible security solutions. In the article by El Bansarkhani et al., the authors present two concepts that contribute to securing emergent business applications: reputation-based trust mechanisms and secure data aggregation.

Part III on Agile Software Development is introduced by Boes and Kämpf from ISF Munich. For a long time, agile methods such as Scrum, XP, Pair Programming, or Test-Driven Development have been considered as an innovative niche for specialists in IT. Today this changed profoundly and agile methods have made their way on a large scale into the IT world. They are now being applied area wide, even in the big companies, e.g., Google, IBM, Microsoft, SAP, and Software AG.

The combination of agile methods and the principles of lean development has become the foundation for a deep change in the organization of software development in general. Empowered teams, synchronized development processes, collective forms of knowledge, and continuous improvement of processes are the central elements of the new state-of-the-art in software development. This evolving organization of work in the IT sector leads to a new situation for IT employees and to new working conditions. Based on empirical research Boes and Kämpf show how the work of software developers has changed, which experiences they have made, and which challenges they are confronted with.

Schnitter and Geppert from SAP AG and Software AG, respectively, argue that the introduction of agile software development methods requires a significant change of the mindset toward openness, honesty, and flexibility. Therefore, the adoption of agile development by the industry is also a process of cultural change that takes a long time and surfaces many issues which so far have been neglected or hidden with other development models.

Adoption of agile practices in global companies has consequences. In their article, Schnitter and Geppert report about their observations related to large-scale agile software development that demands a management style focusing on constant learning and communication, a certain degree of up-front planning to support agility and emergent design, and in-depth examination of software development practices. They consider agile development methods as a toolbox with useful tools for all software development phases.

In the following two articles, the reader is informed about the experiences made at Software AG and SAP AG when agile and lean software development methods were introduced. First, Kampfmann reports on how these methods helped Software AG to progress from unpredictable release schedules to in-time delivery, and from unclear product and feature status to transparent backlog status. The case scenario is the webMethods division of Software AG. She highlights the positive effects on developments spanning multiple teams and on the formation of a comprehensive assembly line for building and testing complex product suites, implementing continuous integration, and delivery.

Likewise, Heymann and Kampfmann report about the deep changes agile methods meant to SAP AG affecting, for instance, the setup of teams, the way these teams work, and the understanding of roles and responsibilities. They motivate why SAP AG introduced agile software development, give insights on how SAP train their software developers, and share the lessons they learned in this process.

This volume is completed by a contribution of Happe et al. from Karlsruhe Institute of Technology (KIT) about software performance engineering, which supports software architects in identifying potential performance problems in software systems during the design phase. Details of the implementation and execution environment of a system are crucial for accurate performance predictions. Yet, only little information about these details is available during early stages of the software life cycle; furthermore, model-based architectural description languages used by software architects are lacking support for performance-relevant information. Therefore, architectural models need to be extended to meta-models to be ready to include design details as they become available when development advances.

Happe et al. report on their experiences with a variety of meta-model extension techniques for business software performance engineering, covering completions, direct invasive techniques, decorator models, and profiles for model-driven performance engineering. In their article, they also report about a case study with the extension of a component-based system that illustrates the benefit of performance completions with respect to the accuracy of performance predictions.

The authors of the articles in this volume are connected via research projects in the German Software-Cluster (www.software-cluster.org), a network of world-leading companies and research institutions concerned with business software innovations. These projects are co-funded by the German Federal Ministry for Education and Research. It is the hope of the editors that this volume stimulates a fruitful dialog between practitioners and researchers about the challenges in the field of business software.

Gino Brunetti
Thomas Feld
Lutz Heuser
Joachim Schnitter
Christian Webel

collective forms of knowledge, and continuous improvement of processes are the central elements of the new state-of-the-art in software development. This evolving organization of work in the IT sector leads to a new situation for IT employees and to new working conditions. Based on empirical research Boes and Kämpf show how the work of software developers has changed, which experiences they have made, and which challenges they are confronted with.

Schnitter and Geppert from SAP AG and Software AG, respectively, argue that the introduction of agile software development methods requires a significant change of the mindset toward openness, honesty, and flexibility. Therefore, the adoption of agile development by the industry is also a process of cultural change that takes a long time and surfaces many issues which so far have been neglected or hidden with other development models.

Adoption of agile practices in global companies has consequences. In their article, Schnitter and Geppert report about their observations related to large-scale agile software development that demands a management style focusing on constant learning and communication, a certain degree of up-front planning to support agility and emergent design, and in-depth examination of software development practices. They consider agile development methods as a toolbox with useful tools for all software development phases.

In the following two articles, the reader is informed about the experiences made at Software AG and SAP AG when agile and lean software development methods were introduced. First, Kampfmann reports on how these methods helped Software AG to progress from unpredictable release schedules to in-time delivery, and from unclear product and feature status to transparent backlog status. The case scenario is the webMethods division of Software AG. She highlights the positive effects on developments spanning multiple teams and on the formation of a comprehensive assembly line for building and testing complex product suites, implementing continuous integration, and delivery.

Likewise, Heymann and Kampfmann report about the deep changes agile methods meant to SAP AG affecting, for instance, the setup of teams, the way these teams work, and the understanding of roles and responsibilities. They motivate why SAP AG introduced agile software development, give insights on how SAP train their software developers, and share the lessons they learned in this process.

This volume is completed by a contribution of Happe et al. from Karlsruhe Institute of Technology (KIT) about software performance engineering, which supports software architects in identifying potential performance problems in software systems during the design phase. Details of the implementation and execution environment of a system are crucial for accurate performance predictions. Yet, only little information about these details is available during early stages of the software life cycle; furthermore, model-based architectural description languages used by software architects are lacking support for performance-relevant information. Therefore, architectural models need to be extended to meta-models to be ready to include design details as they become available when development advances.

Business Process Management (BPM) is the next important issue related to the emergent software systems discussed in this volume. Feld and Hoffmann from the Scheer Group argue that nowadays managers are facing a fast-moving business environment with changing customer needs and expectations, fast-evolving technologies and product lifecycles, strong globalization effects, accelerating innovation, and increasing digitization of products. Within this environment, managers need to ensure long-term business success for their company. In a growing market, it is important to respond by investing in innovative new products, sales channels, and marketing strategies.

Organizations operating in a tough economic environment also need to focus on optimizing costs, timescales, and product resources in order to boost efficiency. According to Feld and Hoffmann, long-term business success is all about the ability of an organization to respond quickly to the changing market conditions, adapting their business model, and bringing their market strategy to operational execution through appropriate business processes, people, and technologies. BPM is essential to ensure this long-term business success based on flexible, market-responsive structures that simultaneously promote efficiency. The challenge is the management of individualized process variants. The authors therefore introduce process on demand as an extended methodology for BPM and the implementation of business processes that enables a flexible and rapid adoption.

The part about emergent software as main characteristic of future business software solutions is rounded up by the aspect of IT security. Cross-company emergent business models can only be successful if they are trusted. This implies that they have an adequate level of security. Important security features include the ability to identify components and their properties to reliably verify the correct functioning of services, while protecting the privacy of individuals, organizations, and businesses properly. The properties of components and services and the protection goals for the data must be specified in order to enforce the appropriate security features at the various levels of the system.

Emergent business software is highly dynamic and flexible. Monolithic security solutions cannot secure the service composites that this new paradigm enables. Instead, different security services have to be combined in order to provide flexible security solutions. In the article by El Bansarkhani et al., the authors present two concepts that contribute to securing emergent business applications: reputation-based trust mechanisms and secure data aggregation.

Part III on Agile Software Development is introduced by Boes and Kämpf from ISF Munich. For a long time, agile methods such as Scrum, XP, Pair Programming, or Test-Driven Development have been considered as an innovative niche for specialists in IT. Today this changed profoundly and agile methods have made their way on a large scale into the IT world. They are now being applied area wide, even in the big companies, e.g., Google, IBM, Microsoft, SAP, and Software AG.

The combination of agile methods and the principles of lean development has become the foundation for a deep change in the organization of software development in general. Empowered teams, synchronized development processes,

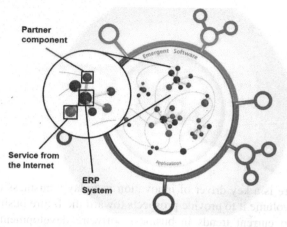

Fig. 1 The emergent software paradigm

multiple providers. This means emergent software will be relatively easy to maintain and, furthermore, will not require significant investments for integration on user side. Users will therefore be able to increase the flexibility of their new and innovative business models, operate them in a more market-oriented manner, and map them within their software systems.

One challenge addressed by Rombach et al. from the Fraunhofer Institute for Experimental Software Engineering (IESE) is how to measure the impact of emergent software, i.e., how to determine the benefit of these methodological and technological solutions with regard to business goals. This requires a goal-oriented measurement approach encompassing the definition of measurement goals, the definition of metrics, and the interpretation of the measured data in the underlying context. Their contribution to this book outlines an approach for quantitatively evaluating the techniques and tools developed to measure the impact of emergence in business applications.

The article by Kleeberg et al. from the SEEBURGER AG analyzes current practices and upcoming trends of information systems integration in the context of cloud computing technology. Therefore, cloud integration scenarios and related challenges from multiple perspectives are discussed. Modern enterprise IT landscapes increasingly include best-of-breed business applications, platforms, and infrastructure sourced on demand from cloud service providers. Such IT cloud sourcing fosters both scalability and flexibility of enterprise information systems, which enables fast responses to ever-changing market needs and competition.

However, cloud computing also extends the need for information systems integration on the levels of data, components, and processes, also beyond the boundaries of a single enterprise. Furthermore, integration technology providers increasingly offer their solutions as-a-service in the cloud, which allows them to extend their portfolios in response to technology trends like big data or mobile outreach. Kleeberg et al. also draw a vision of a cloud-based integration technology stack that enables a wide range of federated cloud integration solutions.

Foreword

Business software is a key driver of innovation in today's business environment. The aim of this volume it to provide prospects toward the future business software and insights into current trends in business software development. The target audience are software developers, IT practitioners, and researchers from the domains business software, security, cloud computing, software technology, and related domains.

The volume is organized into three parts. In Part I, Fischer and Jost from SAP AG and Software AG, the two largest German software houses and international key players in the business software segment, provide their views on emerging business networks, the potential for business software behind the cloud technology, and the future of business software. Part II about emergent software introduces the characteristics of the next generation of business software. Part III about agile software development addresses new trends in software development and provides insights about respective strategies and experiences of SAP AG and Software AG.

The new paradigm of emergent software addresses the highly complex requirements of tomorrow's business software. It aims at dynamically and flexibly combining a multiplicity of components from various providers and adapting itself more easily to new market or business requirements without major efforts for software integration. A wide range of different services is increasingly offered and used in the Internet via cloud platforms in a cost-effective and efficient way (see Fig. 1). In this environment, emergent software is an approach to fulfill the highly complex requirements of digital companies, i.e., companies that have digitalized most or all of their business processes such that business software becomes the decisive driver behind product and process innovation.

Emergent software can adapt itself dynamically to the changing requirements of the market as well as the business environment and supports service relationships between companies. The intelligent linking of existing offers and the addition of supplementary components and services allows a completely new range of services to be provided.

Companies that make use of emergent software will be able to realize new business models—models that would have been unthinkable during the original development of the components and services. Users of emergent software receive individual solutions via the simple composition of standard solutions from

Happe et al. report on their experiences with a variety of meta-model extension techniques for business software performance engineering, covering completions, direct invasive techniques, decorator models, and profiles for model-driven performance engineering. In their article, they also report about a case study with the extension of a component-based system that illustrates the benefit of performance completions with respect to the accuracy of performance predictions.

The authors of the articles in this volume are connected via research projects in the German Software-Cluster (www.software-cluster.org), a network of world-leading companies and research institutions concerned with business software innovations. These projects are co-funded by the German Federal Ministry for Education and Research. It is the hope of the editors that this volume stimulates a fruitful dialog between practitioners and researchers about the challenges in the field of business software.

Gino Brunetti
Thomas Feld
Lutz Heuser
Joachim Schnitter
Christian Webel

Contents

Part I
Trends in Business Software

Emerging Business Networks and the Future of Business Software

Stephan Fischer

Abstract This paper introduces the term *real-time value-add networks* as the IT backbone of emerging business networks in a hyper-connected world. Two research topics are presented that show core aspects of the future of enterprise computing. Rapid Application Development can be used to implement new business processes easily and quickly across heterogeneous cloud platforms and business networks. Secure multi-party computing enables business networks to optimize processes across organizational boundaries without revealing business-critical data. Both research topics show the challenges on the way towards the future of business software and the relevance of innovation communities.

1 Introduction

IT paradigms usually follow two main lines of arguments, either starting with a broader technology vision or with current societal changes. Paradigms that address long-living visions show a clear direction trying to bring them step by step into reality. Progress is made by always using the latest technologies at hand and trying to close the gap between vision and reality. IT paradigms that are based on societal changes use mid-term trends in business and society and translate them into the language of computer scientists, application developers, and business executives. This paper aims to discuss the trends that lie behind today's disruptive innovations. The future business software is tightly connected with social networks that have emerged and are entering the business world rapidly. What will the business world look like in the mid-term future? What IT will be needed? The Internet will surely continue to be one of the drivers of change. Ten years ago, the business world

S. Fischer (✉)
TIP Strategic Innovation, SAP AG, Walldorf, Germany
e-mail: s.fischer@sap.com

G. Brunetti et al. (eds.), *Future Business Software*,
Progress in IS, DOI: 10.1007/978-3-319-04144-5_1,
© Springer International Publishing Switzerland 2014

3

discussed whether the Internet will ever be a viable channel of business (Ariba Inc. 2012). Meanwhile, the Internet has evolved into a backbone of society and business, already called a societal operating system (Couturier et al. 2011). It is one of the driving forces of productivity and profitability, together with technologies such as cloud computing, mobile computing, and in-memory computing.

We will use the term *real-time value-add networks* to explain the new quality that future business software will need in order to serve the companies' needs. This term contains elements of both aforementioned traditions of IT paradigms. *Real-time* has been at the core of SAP's solutions from the very beginning—reflected in the famous "R" in the early product names (Kagermann 2004). Providing real-time insights into business processes and data turned out to be a long-time vision that led to a series of innovations in business software. It is also a force behind SAP's in-memory database and platform, SAP HANA®. The term *value-add networks* is different. Its starting point is a global trend that had been recognized already more than a decade ago: The world is becoming more and more connected. We will soon live in a hyper-connected world of humans and things, full of sensors, smart devices and connected machines. Businesses will become more and more flexible and adaptive, boundaries between organizations will disappear, and a new kind of business, the networked enterprise, emerges (Bughin and Chui 2010). *Real-time value-add networks* will be the inter-organizational set-up facing these trends.

This paper lays out this vision in three steps. First, the term *hyper-connected world* will be introduced. Second, we review the business requirements for companies that would like to enter the *hyper-connected world*. We will then introduce the term *real-time value-add networks* and present current research in enterprise software, including research on emergent software. In addition to software, future networked businesses need open ecosystems to enable innovation, which is the main message and conclusion of this paper.

2 Hyper-Connected Worlds

Globalization has been one of the major trends for businesses in the past decade. It enabled unexpected growth and wealth for some regions, but it also brought challenges for other regions. Companies learnt quickly that technology has always played an important role both as a driver for globalization and as an enabler for companies to innovate, strengthen, and grow their business.

In 2005, the publicist Friedman (2007) introduced a new and influential term to describe the effects of technologies on the globalization of business and competition: *The World is Flat* reads the book title of Friedman's then much-discussed bestseller. He argued that the world has changed into a playing field providing individuals from all regions of the world with equal opportunities to offer their work and services globally. The shift has been driven by so-called "flatteners"—most of them are new technologies that removed unevenness from the business world and introduced a much stronger competition across the world. This includes the invention of the Web browser in the 1990s, search engines, tools for online communication and collaboration, outsourcing, and off-shoring. When Friedman revisited the topic 7 years later, he described the globalization even more dramatically: Products and services are "made in the world" (Friedman 2012). Products can be imagined, designed, marketed, and built through global supply chains and sold everywhere. The world has become even flatter.

The metaphor of a flat world catches well the fact that globalization is a driving force bringing dramatic changes to today's businesses—and that these changes can hardly be avoided. However, experts find the term *flat world* misleading for two reasons. Some critics argue that the world might have become flatter in some aspects, but not on a global scale. In some cases, the world has become even less flat, as the economist Stiglitz (2006) writes in his book "Making Globalization Work". Developing countries could not participate in global business, and their disadvantage seems rather to increase. The term *flat world* is also seen as misleading since it does not show a more relevant change: The world has rather become more connected, as Stiglitz points out (2006, p. 57).

The term *connected world* fits well into today's world of social media such as *Facebook* and *Twitter*. The term explains aptly the new quality of information awareness and exchange that the so-called flatteners brought to us, as most of them provide people and businesses with new means to connect with each other. This is exactly what the *connected world* term was introduced for by the philosopher Manuel Castells. He aimed to describe societies that heavily rely on IT technologies to connect individuals and to build social networks (Castells 2000). Today, large parts of our economy are based on IT technologies that provide a platform for doing business, which led to terms and concepts like "networked economy" (Ariba Inc. 2012) and "networked enterprise" (Bughin and Chui 2010). These concepts reflect the fact that cloud computing and social technologies allow companies to collaborate more and more efficiently. Organizational borders seem to vanish. As a consequence, the ability to coordinate processes and to optimize collaboration within business networks and communities has become a clear competitive advantage.

Interestingly, the current decade gave birth to a new paradigm called *hyper-connected world* that integrates both the *flat world* and the *connected world* metaphor (Timmons 2013). It reflects the increasing efficiency and competition in global business as well as a new quality of connectedness we experience when talking about today's society.

The concept of a *hyper-connected world* adds two important aspects. The first aspect is the pervasive connectivity through cloud computing, mobile connectivity, and connected devices of any kinds (Settembre 2012). One billion users are active in social online networks today. By 2020, around 50 billion devices will be part of the network, such as smart phones, sensors, and actors (Ericsson 2011). Smart items will be part of our real and virtual worlds. They will create a treasure trove of data which will enable new business services. New kinds of intelligent tools will be created that help knowledge workers but will also compete with—"a bigger pool of cheap geniuses—some of whom are people and some are now robots, microchips and software-guided machines", as Friedman put it (2011).

The second aspect of the *hyper-connected world* is emergence—a term lent from biology. It describes a characteristic of complex systems that contain several levels and subsystems influencing each other in a way that cannot be foreseen in advance. This is exactly the case for many of today's organizations that exist within "networks of networks, unable to completely control any of them", as Gartner says (Austin 2012).

The *hyper-connected world* evolves from a broad digitalization, sensorization, robotics, and pervasive connectivity for humans and devices. The Internet will become a network of almost everything. Any item can become a smart item and any service a web-based service and will be integrated into business processes and our daily life. As a consequence, every service, item, and data stream can be monetized, and the same will be true for human activities, be it work or the value of a customer as an individual consumer. Network-based businesses will become the primary source of economic growth. Open innovation and crowd sourcing will be key drivers for business success. Innovative companies will quickly recognize new demands and market opportunities and will quickly adjust to be ahead of the competition. Successful companies will work with highly flexible, often temporary structures, for example with freelancers and short-term partnerships. Value chains will become value networks, continuously being restructured, sometimes disruptively.

The *connected world* metaphor was used to highlight online tools that enabled people to interact freely, exchange ideas and collaborate without borders. In the *hyper-connected world*, businesses seek to have similar platforms to interact with others and to integrate services, products, and processes on a global scale. Platforms and aggregators that orchestrate flexibility and emergent structures across companies and industries will be crucial for the *hyper-connected world*. This leads to the core topic of this paper, namely emerging business networks and the future of business software.

3 Future of Business in Real-Time Value-Add Networks

The *hyper-connected world* creates a number of requirements for businesses and their IT backbones. Business activities will be organized more and more in *real-time value-add networks* in the future—a term that combines the real-time paradigm known from the enterprise resource planning (ERP) world with the notion of creating value within and from networks.

3.1 Factories of the Future

The manufacturing industry is an example where business and technology trends already show characteristics of the hyper-connected world. For more than four decades, the information and communication technologies (ICT) have helped to optimize production processes, but experts see a new quality of technologies and business opportunities coming up. This new world of manufacturing will heavily influence our industrial society and is being shaped by national and international initiatives such as the *Industrie 4.0* initiative in the context of the German High-Tech Strategy (Forschungsunion 2011). The business climate for manufacturers has changed during the last years. Cost pressure has further increased as well as market volatility. Product lifecycles are becoming shorter and customers start to demand individualized products in growing numbers. Companies therefore seek for more flexible processes and more dynamic supply chains as well as the possibility to implement rapid prototyping and testing of new products, one-piece flows and mass customization, to name a few. Flexibility can be reached with Internet of Things technologies that bridge the gap between the real world and enterprise systems. Sensors and smart items produce large data flows that allow real-time analysis of processes, products, quality, and cost, integrating the real world much better into the virtual world of production and logistics systems. This enables automatic detection of errors, quality issues or changes in demand, followed by faster decisions thanks to predictive analytics and transparency of needed and available capacities. The factories of the future will adapt automatically to changes, will increase or lower capacities according to the demand, will allow ad-hoc reconfigurations and customized products. The supply chains of the future will show features that are in some respect chaotic since they can no longer be controlled through predefined processes. Instead they will be managed through real-time monitoring and feedback as well as dynamic process negotiation across the network in order to adapt logistic processes, business relationships and production.

3.2 Five Core Characteristics

The manufacturing example illustrates five core characteristics of *real-time value-add networks* in a *hyper-connected world*:

Interlinked processes. Business processes will be interlinked through the whole life cycle—including design, prototyping, test, configuration, planning and production.

Value network optimization. Enterprises will not only optimize their business within their own organizational borders; the whole business network will be optimized, which will lead to a much higher value for all members of the business network. Some optimizations can be realized with classical methods, now applied for a group of companies within a network. Other optimizations will happen through emergence due to new flexibility provided by emergent software and other concepts.

Monitoring in real-time. Digitalization and pervasive connectivity will enable real-time analysis of all business activities, covering business relationships, production, logistics and any other processes.

Adaptations in real-time. Businesses will use their knowledge from real-time monitoring and change their business processes and objectives surprisingly fast; decisions are made to anticipate changes, react to changes in customer behavior or market conditions, or to disrupt the business with new business ideas.

Highly dynamic. Businesses must be able to manage dynamic, sometimes disruptive changes in several dimensions. Companies will continue to engage in long-living business networks, but more and more business will be done in short-term networks. Some networks will consist of big companies, others of a mixture of large and small partners as well as individual contributors. Value-adding processes will be negotiated dynamically along these networks, taking into account quality, time, price, viability, sustainability, and any other dimension relevant for the network. These dynamics of business processes will lead to an increase of outsourcing; projects and tasks will be broken down into micro activities. Orchestrators will take over the coordination.

3.3 IT Requirements

Today's large scale enterprise software systems are by far not flexible enough to support *real-time value-add networks*. Current system landscapes have evolved over the years. They combine a variety of systems and modules that mostly have been enhanced and customized for a set of predefined processes. They are optimized, but the optimization focuses mostly on one enterprise and not the whole business network. Their flexibility is bound to the design-time and implementation projects. That is the reason why they appear to be rather static.

In contrast, the IT requirements of the new kind of business networks are highly demanding. Businesses need platforms that work across many different types of devices (including sensors), that provide automatically generated data and monitoring, that allow tracking of task completion and quality assessments across organizations, and enable pricing and revenue sharing models, as well as data security in business networks. All this can be summarized as an adaptability that goes way beyond design-time changes since it allows systems to change intra- and inter-company processes in business real-time. This system behavior has also been called emergence since it allows the software to evolve and adapt based on a stable core, creating new processes, rules and standards that can neither be designed nor foreseen in advance (Frischbier et al. 2012).

4 Research Questions

The German research cluster "Software-Cluster", located in South-West Germany, is devoted to emergent software as a research topic (Software-Cluster 2013a). Several research projects develop concepts and prototypes for "digital companies", which are companies that digitize more and more processes. Digital companies need enterprise software that is highly flexible to compete in a hyper-connected world. This flexibility can be provided by emergent structures. Emergent software is designed to combine a wide range of components from different manufacturers in a dynamic and flexible manner, in order to fulfill the highly complex requirements of digitalized companies. The vision includes that such software can adapt itself dynamically to the changing requirements of the market as well as the business environment and supports service relationships between companies (Software-Cluster 2013b). Emergent structures are one building block for *real-time value-add networks*.

4.1 An Architectural View on Emergent Software

From a technical point of view, *real-time value-add networks* will definitely use cloud infrastructures for collaboration, application development, deployment, process orchestration, and data fusion. We assume that the architecture will consist of a general infrastructure layer (Infrastructure-as-a-Service) that serves as a basis for tools and services for developers which are provided by a second layer (Platform-as-a-Service) on top of the infrastructure. A third layer is above the cloud platform and infrastructure layers and consists of components, services, and tools that allow developers to create applications with emergent features. This layer might include data processing and mining tools, reputation management, metering, billing, service bundling and many others. New application scenarios can be realized by combining these components with business processes on the top level, which is foreseen as a layer for Business-Process-as-a-Service. All layers must ensure interoperability and adaptability which are main challenges of today's architectures. An additional, more general challenge is today's heterogeneous system landscape. Business processes will make use of services from several heterogeneous cloud platforms and will operate across organizational and system boundaries. This needs to be taken into account when developing reference architectures for emergent software, which is done in the research project *EMERGENT* of the Software-Cluster (2013b).

We will use the aforementioned architectural view on *real-time value-add networks* to highlight two research questions that SAP has worked on in the past. Research can help to explain how a transition from the current software systems to future emergent software systems and *real-time value-add networks* could look like. SAP has been engaged in several research projects along paradigms of real-time and business networks. We present two of them, rapid application development and privacy-preserving multi-party computing.

4.2 Rapid Application Development

In the 1990s, software experts felt that the software development process was in general too slow and too rigid to adjust to changing requirements or business needs. At this time, practitioners proposed several new software development concepts that promised to make software development more flexible. Agile software development is one of these concepts. It focuses on the development process rather than the software code and has been widely adopted in the industry (Schnitter and Geppert 2013, in this volume). One core idea is to have software written in short intervals which allows software developers to enhance the software incrementally and continuously, as well as to assess risks and a change of the focus and requirements of a software project.

The rapid application development (RAD) method is another, promising technique to speed up development. Its focus lies on tools for prototyping that allow developers to test software features fast and to get end user feedback as early as possible (Martin 1991). One of RAD's core ideas is to have a set of platform-independent tools and techniques that developers can use to create running prototypes within only days or hours.

Seen from the needs of members of a *real-time value-add network*, the flexibility of RAD envisions a core requirement for fast responses to ad-hoc business needs. Usually, the implementation of a new business process is time-consuming work. The first step is to create a concept and model of the needed business process. This is conducted by business and IT experts of partner companies in the business network. In a second step, the new or enhanced process is being implemented. In most cases, this leads to the development of new software which typically is a highly manual task. In addition, companies in a network may use different and often proprietary platforms. On-boarding of new developers can be rather time consuming, and developing and deploying new services may need specific know-how or require learning.

A main research question is how software artifacts for heterogeneous cloud platforms can be created automatically based on the process model the experts developed beforehand. Rapid application development already offers tools that allow automated code generation on a target platform. The research project *InDiNet* (Innovative Services for the Internet of the Future) allowed us to experiment with this idea (Software-Cluster 2013c). Researchers from SAP used a common RAD tool—*Spring Roo*—and enhanced it by developing add-ons that generate code for cloud platforms. The project work is based on the SAP HANA Cloud Platform as an exemplary cloud platform.

The outcome is a much more comfortable way to kick-start web applications development based on the SAP HANA Cloud Platform. *Spring Roo* is a tool and framework that helps to create basic web applications in minutes. Developers only need to define a data model of the web application. The tool automatically creates backend and frontend applications that cover the most important features like persistency, create, read, update, and delete. *Spring Roo* is widely used, especially by small and medium companies. One team within the research project *InDiNet* created add-ons for *Spring Roo* that allow developers to easily configure apps for the SAP HANA Cloud Platform, deploy them and start or stop instances of it. A third add-on helps to create SAP UI5-based web frontends for these apps. This tool ensemble enables developers to prepare a skeleton application quickly and test it on the cloud platform. After a basic application is created, the developers can start to enrich the application by solely focusing on business logic. Knowledge about platform specifics is not needed. This has been demonstrated in the *InDiNet* project when researchers created a backend prototype for a logistics app that uses services from several cloud platforms.

4.3 Secure Multi-party Computing

Collaboration within business networks offers great opportunities. Joint decision making across organizations can reduce cost of business processes and improve quality and performance. Supply chain optimization is a well-known example. Usually, companies optimize processes within their own area of control, mostly their organizational borders. This leads to supply chains whose process steps are locally optimized by individual companies. It is a well-acknowledged fact that the companies in a supply chain would benefit more from a global optimum that takes into account data from all members of the supply chain, for example cost and capacity data, inventory levels, and demand forecast. Almost all companies decide not to disclose this information, since it is seen as business critical. Sharing this information can impose huge disadvantages for a supply chain member, as disclosed cost data can be used by customers to enforce lower prices (Pibernik et al. 2011).

Research has focused on several security aspects of the *grid problem*, which is the scientific term for the challenge of secure resource sharing among a dynamic network of organizations. One aspect is the system architecture that enables companies within a virtual organization to share data in a secure way, for example by access control and ensuring execution integrity (Kerschbaum and Robinson 2009).

In addition, we would like to stress a second line of research that is done by SAP and partners. Cryptography can provide businesses with an elegant solution of the grid problem. It is the main idea to encrypt the data from the companies before centrally computing the optimum of a supply chain or any other business process within the network. Mathematical methods ensure that the optimization works with encrypted data and that the results can be decrypted, and can offer the network parties insights about how they need to contribute to the optimization. Transforming business-critical data into encrypted data ensures that no member of the network discloses the critical information to others.

Interestingly, the idea of secure multi-party computing was already proposed back in the 1980s (Ben-Or et al. 1988). However, early algorithms had a low computational performance and could not be used in a real world setting from a practical point of view. Research has shown that special cases of the optimization problem can be solved efficiently with a novel privacy-preserving transformation. This is the case for privacy-preserving multiparty Linear Programming (LP), a special case of an optimization algorithm (Dreier and Kerschbaum 2011), and other cases of supply chain collaboration. This ground work is the basis of several opportunities multi-party computing can generate, from benchmarking within business networks to quality and reputation management.

5 Conclusion: Enabling Open Ecosystems and Innovation Communities

Software will be a key element in a *hyper-connected world*. Both technology and business trends will force companies to innovate in order to stay competitive. This is a challenge individual companies can hardly meet when only using their own strengths. More and more value will be created within networks of large and small companies and not within the borders of an individual company. These networks must be able to react dynamically to changes in business conditions and adjust business processes fast and smoothly according to the business requirements. These emerging business networks need an appropriate IT backbone, which leads us to the term *real-time value-add business networks*. We reviewed a possible architecture of the underlying cloud platforms, components, apps and services and showed how current research projects contribute to a transition from present enterprise software systems to the future business software organized in cross-company networks.

The term *real-time value-add business networks* leverages two paradigms. Both were visible in the examples we provided: The vision of real-time computing for enterprises is still a main driver for research and development. We reviewed the paradigm for business networks and, as a consequence, broadened its meaning. The real-time paradigm does not only mean to provide access to business data in real-time. It also means to create or change business processes fast (and ideally in real-time). This goal of real-time business process restructuring cannot be reached easily, as it is rather a vision, but the example of *rapid application development* shows that the real-time paradigm continues to be productive and a strong motivation for further research. This is where *real-time value-add business networks* meet the vision of emergent software.

The term *value-add business networks* reflects the rise of social computing and will drive its adoption within the business world. Privacy-preserving multi-party computing is an example of how IT can help to create value in future business networks. The example also demonstrates what ground work is still needed to bring enterprise computing to the next level; applied research can provide the right software solutions for the challenges of a hyper-connected world.

A second learning is that businesses will rely even more on software systems, cloud computing, web-based services, and ICT in general in the future. Platforms and ecosystems will play a mission-critical role. Open platforms and developer ecosystems will become more and more important as businesses will become more and more collaborative. The world might become flatter, more connected, even hyper-connected, but it is definitely becoming more challenging for businesses. We can prepare ourselves for this challenging future by collaborating in research and development, by pursuing open ecosystems, common test beds for prototyping and market trials. The notion of *real-time value-add networks* reminds us that businesses live in ecosystems and that trusted partners count—no matter their size, industry, or region. Co-innovation with customers and partners was one of the key elements for SAP to grow into the world leader in business software, and this will stay true in a *hyper-connected world* and emerging *real-time value-add business networks* in the future.

References

Ariba Inc. (2012) The networked economy. Sunnyvale

Austin T (2012) Viewpoint: gartner on the changing nature of work. In: BBC news business. http://www.bbc.co.uk/news/business-16968125. Accessed 18 Feb 2013

Ben-Or M, Goldwasser S, Widgerson A (1988) Completeness theorems for non-cryptographic fault-tolerant distributed computation. In: Proceedings of the 20th ACM symposium on theory of computing, Chicago, 2–4 May 1988

Bughin J, Chui M (2010) The rise of the networked enterprise: web 2.0 finds its payday. Mac Kinsey Q—Online J Mc Kinsey Company http://www.mckinseyquarterly.com/article_print. aspx?L2=18&L3=30&ar=2716. Accessed 18 Feb 2013

Castells M (2000) The information age: economy, society, and culture. In: The rise of the network society, vol 1. Blackwell Publishing, Oxford

Couturier H, Neidecker-Lutz B, Schmidt V, Woods D (2011) Understanding the future internet. Evolved Media, New York

Dreier J, Kerschbaum F (2011) Practical privacy-preserving multiparty linear programming based in problem transformation. Paper presented at the 3rd IEEE international conference on privacy, security, risk and trust (PASSAT), 9–11 Oct 2011

Ericsson (2011) More than 50 billion connected devices, Stockholm

Forschungsunion (2011) Bericht der Promotorengruppe Kommunikation. Im Fokus: Das Zukunftsprojekt Industrie 4.0. Handlungsempfehlungen zur Umsetzung. http://www. forschungsunion.de/pdf/kommunikation_bericht_2012.pdf. Accessed 18 Feb 2013

Friedman T (2007) The world is flat. The globalized world in the twenty-first century. Penguin Books, London

Friedman T (2011) How did the robot end up with my job? In: The New York Times. http://www. nytimes.com/2011/10/02/opinion/sunday/friedman-how-did-the-robot-end-up-with-my-job. html?_r=0. Accessed 18 Feb 2013

Friedman T (2012) Made in the world. In: The New York Times. The Sunday Review. http:// www.nytimes.com/2012/01/29/opinion/sunday/friedman-made-in-the-world.html?_r=0. Accessed 18 Feb 2013

Frischbier S, Gesmann M, Mayer D, Roth A, Webel C (2012) Emergence as competitive advantage—engineering tomorrow's enterprise software systems. In: Proceedings of the 14th international conference on enterprise information systems (ICEIS 2012), Wroclaw, Poland, 28 Jun–1 Jul 2012

Kagermann H (ed) (2004) Real time: a tribute to Hasso Plattner. Wiley, Indianapolis

Kerschbaum F, Robinson P (2009) Security architecture for virtual organizations of business web services. J Syst Architect 55(4):224–232

Martin J (1991) Rapid application development. Macmillan, New York

Pibernik R, Yingying Z, Kerschbaum F, Schröpfer A (2011) Secure collaborative supply chain planning and inverse optimization—the JELS model. Eur J Oper Res 208:75–85

Schnitter J, Geppert J (2013) Agile software development—what is left to do? In: Brunetti G, Feld T, Schnitter J, Webel C, Heuser L (ed) Future business software. Springer, Berlin, Heidelberg (in this book)

Settembre M (2012) Towards a hyper-connected world. In: 2012 XVth international telecommunications network strategy and planning symposium (NETWORKS), 15–18 Oct 2012 doi:10.1109/NETWKS.2012.6381667

Software-Cluster (2013a) http://www.software-cluster.com/en/. Accessed 18 Feb 2013

Software-Cluster (2013b) http://www.software-cluster.com/en/research/topics/emergent-software . Accessed 18 Feb 2013

Software-Cluster (2013c) http://www.software-cluster.org/en/research/projects/joint-projects/ indinet. Accessed 18 Feb 2013

Stiglitz J (2006) Making globalization work. W W Norton & Company Inc., New York, London

Timmons H (2013) Thomas Friedman answers your questions. In: The New York Times. India Ink. http://india.blogs.nytimes.com/2013/02/18/thomas-friedman-answers-your-questions/? Accessed 18 Feb 2013

Collaborative and Social: The Real Potential Behind the Cloud

Wolfram Jost

Cloud computing is one of the hottest topics in IT today. Only a few experts understand exactly what it is, and even fewer recognize what a great opportunity it represents in the new business model for work organization.

Consumerization—this neologism is one of the biggest challenges facing the computer industry and corporate IT departments in all industries, in the opinion of Gartner, Inc. Each year, the US-based information technology research and advisory company publishes the top 10 strategic technologies. While past lists included such topics as business process management and integration platforms, now we see terms that are familiar from the personal use of computer technology: mobile applications and tablets, social computing, video, advanced analytics, context-aware computing, and the top-ranked cloud computing. Market researchers put all of these under the category of consumerization, which means that fast-spreading devices and services from the private sector are finding their way into the workplace.

This is quite likely the biggest change ever in corporate IT. Consumerization will bring more change with it than did the introduction of personal computers into the workplace, and before that the associated conversion from a mainframe-based infrastructure to more local and flexible client/server architectures in the 80s and 90s. It was this change that motivated the rise of SAP, Oracle, and Sun, not to mention Microsoft with its years-long quasi-monopolistic position in the market for PC operating systems and office software.

Current discussion focuses on the technological developments of cloud computing. The spotlight is on usage-based billing of IT services (also known as "software as a service") and procuring data, programs, and services via the Internet, or "from the cloud." A company's data and programs are stored, organized, and

W. Jost (✉)
Member of the Executive Board, Software AG, Darmstadt, Germany
e-mail: wolfram.jost@softwareag.com

G. Brunetti et al. (eds.), *Future Business Software*,
Progress in IS, DOI: 10.1007/978-3-319-04144-5_2,
© Springer International Publishing Switzerland 2014

15

managed outside the company. Experts portray this model as a major opportunity to save costs, while skeptics focus on the risks associated with virtualization and data backup.

Cloud computing however, is much more. The great thing about cloud computing and all its services is that the technology for managing the programs and data storage remains completely invisible to consumers. The "how" and "where," along with the scaling issues of the IT infrastructure, are of no concern to them. They have virtually limitless access to transparent resources, which are turned on and off in the provider's data center, depending on demand. In other words, in what is probably the most challenging market environment—business with private clients—services are available everywhere around the clock, and good performance is standard. This is regardless of how many users are currently active or newly invited to participate! Anyone familiar with the amount of money and effort involved in an IT department shoving 200 additional users into an application system in a business environment has a great deal of respect for such quality service.

Some of the best known examples for providers of cloud services include Google, Facebook, Amazon, and Apple. These monopolists of consumer IT have organized their IT infrastructure based on the principle of cloud computing, radically changing the way we work, communicate, and act.

Let's take a look at Facebook, for example. In mid-2011, the social media platform claimed to have over 670 million registered members worldwide; in Germany alone there are 20 million users. The company's recipe for success is collaboration and participation. Instead of working in an anonymous Web with search engines and e-mail systems, users receive their own personal content summary ("news feed") from a stream of information sources. In return, they designate friends, reveal preferences, become a "friend" or "fan" of something or someone, and supply their social networks with content.

Google and Amazon focused their services consistently on consumers and their needs, even before Facebook. A Web-enabled smart phone or a PC with Internet access is all a user needs to take advantage of an impressive array of innovative cooperation and collaboration services. Google, for example, offers e-mail, word processing, and spreadsheet programs. The Amazon Cloud Drive is an online hard drive that allows you to store e.g. all your MP3s and access them from any device. Smaller companies and startups are also getting in on the act: Dropbox, based in San Francisco, is another cloud-based file-syncing service that allows users to access and share files from any device.

The new generation starting their careers now takes such high-quality service for granted. Young employees have little understanding for organizational barriers and technical limitations. They are used to being always on and always connected in their personal lives and expect their professional lives to be the same. If they find company-issued devices to be too cumbersome, they don't hesitate to use their personal smart phones, tablet computers, or netbooks. They also use Facebook, Twitter, and other social networking sites to interact and consult with colleagues.

The experiences they have as consumers are a benchmark for them in terms of user friendliness and ease of access, which they use to judge IT services in their professional environments.

1 Consumer Segment Sets the Tone for IT Development

In plain language, this means that the boundaries between personal lives and work are becoming increasingly blurred. The term "consumerization" means that new ideas and innovations arise in the IT world today for the consumer segment rather than specifically for professional use, as in the past. This paradigm shift engages today's CIOs, most of whom came of age in the era of powerful enterprise resource planning (ERP) systems and spent most of their time on integrating and building a secure IT infrastructure.

This generation of IT executives has struggled in recent years, especially with pressure to cut costs and improve efficiency. It's no wonder that their approach to cloud computing focuses primarily on tactical considerations. They connect it with the hope that they can cut operating costs or accelerate the introduction of software-based projects. They also see the appeal in the fact that the business application services can be obtained from the cloud as needed and are billed according to actual usage only.

Analyzing the evolution of corporate IT helps assess the dimensions of cloud computing. A technical innovation always develops its true potential first in conjunction with new business organization models. If one of the two elements is missing, the innovation remains a theoretical construct without practical value. The history of corporate IT is rife with examples of this relationship. Replacing mainframes with the client/server model as the dominant computer architecture can be attributed in part to management's desire to establish divisional or business unit–oriented organizational structures with integrated processes. The triumph of the Internet as a communications infrastructure for businesses is also a result of the division of labor in a globalized economy.

2 Stages of Development for Enterprise Applications

The development of enterprise application software is an impressive reflection of the interplay between technical and organizational progress. For example, the pioneering work of the American consultants Michael Hammer and James Champy on business process reengineering radically changed the perspective on enterprises and their structures and processes. The central idea behind it is that business processes must be rethought from beginning to end in order to eliminate extra costs and wasted time from operations. Finally, one business process combines the basic production factors of labor, land, capital, and information technology with value-added services.

The increased attention to processes has been consistently furthered in the design of highly integrated information systems called enterprise resource planning (ERP) systems. The client/server architecture and the relational database model contributed the necessary technological framework. The boundaries between enterprises that were seen as elemental were made obsolete around the turn of the millennium by the Internet, with its extensive networking and integration capabilities. Furthermore, the companies had to pay for the high degree of integration with a loss of flexibility and agility. The development of customer relationships and the expansion of the value-added chain to include business partners took place in part because of new Internet-compatible application systems integrated into the existing software landscape with the involvement of an additional layer of software (EAI, enterprise application integration).

Companies that entered into a long-term partnership with a leading ERP provider, such as SAP or Oracle, out of a desire to have the most comprehensive support possible for business processes repeatedly come up against this fundamental issue. By providing support for processes all along the services and supply chain, standard programs promise maximum efficiency compared to a combination of special solutions from different providers, but they tend to be inflexible. Against the backdrop of economic momentum that requires ad hoc decisions and a high degree of adaptability in the face of global competition, these systems are more and more troublesome.

Standard application software can be configured for new business processes just to a limited extent, because application function and process control are tightly interwoven with each other. It is time-consuming and expensive for IT specialists to customize the existing software by making any process changes or integrating additional application logic. A high degree of integration has its advantages, but it comes at a cost for companies who lose the agility and flexibility needed in today's dynamic business world. It makes sense to use standard software in areas where processes undergo few changes and/or where competition is not a factor, such as accounting. This does not apply, however, in areas critical to maintaining a competitive advantage, such as marketing, sales, and development, which are subject to constantly changing demands.

In the past, the rigid structures of IT applications have often thwarted creativity in business rather than promoting it. Nowadays solutions are developed using modern software concepts based on comprehensive business process management (BPM) and service-oriented architectures (SOA). The software is separated into services that can be assembled via a process platform as needed without anyone having to manually change the application's code. Separating processing and logic from the application system promises greater agility and flexibility for process configuration, control, and optimization.

3 The Cloud and Processes

Cloud computing will accelerate the BPM and SOA initiatives. Following the model of social networks, it replaces the previous application-centric software design with user-centric process and software development. As a sort of Facebook for processes, cloud-enabled BPM brings business experts and IT specialists together as part of the collaborative model-to-execute approach across organizational and geographic boundaries to work together on improving process models. Operating and IT departments are working in close coordination to develop a common vision for process improvement. Colleagues can be invited to participate short-term, no matter their location. Changes made by one participant are immediately transparent to all participants.

Extreme collaboration—as Gartner calls the new forms of cooperation and collaboration—brings together more people, more expertise, and more information in order to implement business improvements and product innovations. Equipping employees with mobile devices ensures that coordination and decision making take place in real time. Anyone can join in or leave the interaction, at will.

Potential areas of application for such new forms of cooperation can be identified in all layers and levels of a company's business. Manufacturing companies, for example, can now easily establish new innovation processes and invite customers or partners to participate. The Lego company demonstrates the positive effects that this type of participation, also called crowdsourcing, can have. After encountering some grumbling from the web community, the Danish company moved to appease its loyal customers. Interested Lego fans can now access a number of design tools, message boards, etc. to design their own models, publish the model designs for the Lego community, and jointly develop them. Lego is esteemed as a model of successful customer participation. Meanwhile, more and more companies are inviting their customers—or friends, as they are called in the parlance of social networking—to incorporate their ideas, opinions, and wishes into product development.

The new operating and business concepts from the world of social media also take process analysis and modeling out of the realm of specialists. Everything is already in the cloud. Managers do not have to draft a large-scale strategic project and wait for internal procurement and IT to establish the technical requirements. Staff and specialists start of their own accord. The situation is now very straightforward: "Let's write down the process flow and look for improvements." Ad hoc initiatives are started at any time and interested colleagues from around the world are invited, following the model of social networking. The lack of organizational and technological hurdles makes this an excellent, effortless way to gather, compare, and evaluate process designs, ideas, and concepts from the entire company, including the international departments.

With the help of cloud computing, even highly specialized niche providers can establish a collaborative platform on which they complete and refine their product range with the services of other specialists. The advantage of this type of cooperation is that it lowers the entry threshold for new markets significantly. A company in the logistics sector, for instance, no longer must handle all the steps necessary for customs clearance, product tracking, and cold-chain control by itself; it rather can integrate the intelligent services of third parties from the cloud that help complete the logistics process, including all legal requirements.

4 The Cloud Enabled Process Platform

The various models for cooperation and collaboration that make up extreme collaboration form the organizational counterpart to cloud computing. Together they provide real business benefits.

Implementation follows on a process and integration platform that consistently separates process design and control from the application content and has the technical build in feature to fulfill all architectural requirements for operating in the cloud. This fully removes the traditional barriers between the operational and IT departments—one of the key issues in process improvement.

All parties involved in a process, such as the development of a new product, can interact at any time and make suggestions for improvement. This activates all of a company's expertise and, if necessary, that of its network (crowdsourcing). Performance data from monitoring the operational process indicators can be combined as part of collaborative dashboarding and supplemented with comments or explanations. When the market demands change or a new incident arises, ad hoc opinions can be collected from the different management levels and departments in order to jointly reach a decision.

Companies start by introducing a service-oriented architecture (SOA) and business process management (BPM) to achieve improved business and process performance. Daryl C. Plummer, Managing VP and Gartner Fellow, is convinced that extreme collaboration plays a crucial role in the transformation process and in increasing performance. "Cloud computing is speeding up this cooperation. BPM and SOA initiatives develop an even greater impact in that way," the analyst declared.

The combination of BPM, cloud computing, and extreme collaboration will launch a new phase in enterprise software, which again allows for greater customization and flexibility. Business processes are no longer mapped as completely as possible in ERP software; rather, they are controlled as individual process logic blocks outside of the applications. It is beside the point whether the application content is provided by a cloud service or is operating in the traditional system. It is more important that the old IT conflict between standardization and flexibility is resolved, maybe even permanently.

This development will certainly leave a mark for the role of the CIO and his or her IT department within a business organization. The associated consumerization of IT permanently eliminates the traditional position as the supreme ruler of applications and data. The new options fulfill the desire of departmental employees to produce processes themselves, rather than passively waiting for the IT professionals to produce results. The user-centricity which has long been in demand is finally becoming a reality.

This means that CIOs must reinvent themselves and their departments. They can be at the forefront of development and actively support the transformation process. Incentive systems, such as subsidies on the purchase of selected mobile devices and social media contests for the best process design, can accelerate these developments while controlling and directing them. Even with all its advantages, the consumerization of IT is not free of risks. Control and governance are still urgently needed, probably more than ever. Consistency is essential for individual groups' production of processes that need to be combined into an overall process. Even more, it is a matter of a challenge whose controversy is revealed by the heated debate about privacy in social networks. CIOs must find intelligent answers to the question of how to strike a balance between openness, greater participation, and protection of in-house expertise.

Part II
Emergent Software

Measuring the Impact of Emergence in Business Applications

Dieter Rombach, Michael Kläs and Christian Webel

Abstract Enterprise software systems must be designed for flexibility to allow adaptation of their inter-organizational relationships and their products to changing requirements or contexts while retaining existing functionality and user acceptance. To support this, we introduce the notion of Emergent Enterprise Software Systems. Emergent Enterprise Software Systems combine existing software paradigms with proactive and self-x behaviors into a stable and reliable software system. This is mainly achieved via new concepts, methods, tools and technologies. One of the main challenges is how to measure the impact of emergent software, i.e., to determine the benefit of these methodological and technological solutions with regard to business goals. This requires a goal-oriented measurement approach encompassing the definition of measurement goals, the definition of metrics, and the interpretation of measured data in the underlying context. In this paper, we outline a goal-oriented approach (GQM) for quantitatively measuring the impact of emergence enablers, and an approach (GQM+Strategies) for aligning such evaluations across organizational levels.

1 Emergence in Business Software

Nowadays, software markets are characterized by ever shorter time to market and product lifecycles, shared business processes with supply chains across organizations, and combined physical and digital products. In such a context, a competitive

D. Rombach (✉) · M. Kläs · C. Webel
Fraunhofer Institute for Experimental Software Engineering (IESE),
Fraunhofer-Platz 1 67663 Kaiserslautern, Germany
e-mail: dieter.rombach@iese.fraunhofer.de

M. Kläs
e-mail: michael.klaes@iese.fraunhofer.de

C. Webel
e-mail: christian.webel@iese.fraunhofer.de

G. Brunetti et al. (eds.), *Future Business Software*,
Progress in IS, DOI: 10.1007/978-3-319-04144-5_3,
© Springer International Publishing Switzerland 2014

advantage can only be gained by companies that adapt their inter-organizational relationships as well as their products and processes to changing needs. This adaptation has to be quick and must be done (semi-)automatically. Nevertheless, today's enterprise software systems still lack the required level of flexibility and agility needed for this adaptation. With respect to cross-organizational interoperability, these enterprise systems are often designed in a company-centric way with implicitly shared semantics and contexts. Interfaces to external systems are often only available (coarse-grained and high-level) at fixed process steps. Implementing changed requirements or allowing third parties to extend today's systems is hard to do in business real-time. Once designed and implemented, these enterprise systems remain rather static. This limits interoperability and adaptation to being realized at design-time only, forcing a redesign of the system.

To evolve software beyond design-time interoperability and adaptability, we introduce the notion of emergent software (Frischbier et al. 2012). In nature, emergence refers to the development of new behavior in response to changes of the environment based on local perception. Transferred to software, we expect the software system to exhibit new behavior in response to changes of the environment. To be able to do this, the system must be aware of its context and show reactive capabilities. Some of this base functionality has already been developed for self-configuring or self-healing distributed systems. *Emergent Enterprise Software Systems* (*EESS*) must combine existing software paradigms with proactive/reactive behavior and these self-x behaviors into a stable and reliable software system. This is achieved via new concepts, methods, tools, and technologies. One of the main challenges is how to measure the impact of these new solutions, i.e., the impact of emergence in business applications.

2 Technology and Methodology as Enablers for Emergence

In (Frischbier et al. 2012), the arising challenges for emergent systems are discussed from two perspectives: (1) technology and methodology for designing, implementing, and testing, and (2) business process modeling & governance for operating emergent business software. The technological and methodological challenges are mainly addressed in the project EMERGENT, whereas the focus of the project SWINNG is on business processes and models as well as governance. Both are joint research projects of the German Software-Cluster[1] involving both academia and industry.

The technological and methodological challenges within EMERGENT lie in four different research areas: (1) interoperability, (2) adaptivity, (3) usability and user context, and (4) IT security. They are addressed in four corresponding work

---

[1] www.software-cluster.org

packages: The first focuses on finding new concepts, methods, and techniques to provide interoperability on the component and the system level. The work package *Adaptivity* deals with methods and techniques for the dynamic adaptation of heterogeneous information infrastructures across companies and the optimization of (business) processes based on the available resources. *Usability and User Context* deals with the question of how to interact with emergent business software in different and varying user contexts, while *IT Security* focuses on fundamental security-related concepts and technologies in inter-company collaborations.

From a BPM and governance point of view, the main challenges can be classified into three areas: (1) integrating method and tool support for the BPM lifecycle phases; (2) providing holistic governance and compliance methods across distributed organizations, processes, and components; and (3) taking dynamics and unpredictability into account.

First solutions have been implemented in current industry-strength software systems and academic prototypes. This includes new tools, technologies, and software components, but also services and applications.

Now the main problem is that the benefit of the solutions has to be demonstrated in order to

- justify investments, e.g., for development or for redesigning existing systems
- convince customers to use the new emergent software components, and to pay for them
- convince developers so that they trust in the new concepts, methods, and technologies.

In order to be objective, we have to quantify the benefit. The problem is that during data collection, typically too much unnecessary data is collected (since it is sometimes not clear what exactly we have to collect in order to quantify the benefit), a lot of data is not analyzed (since too much data is collected) or, if data is analyzed, it is not analyzed in the right environment. In addition, standard measures are often postulated without adaptation to the environment. As a result, important aspects cannot be analyzed because data is wrong or missing. The consequence is that wrong conclusions may be drawn. So the big challenge is how to measure the impact of emergent software. We propose a goals-oriented measurement approach (GQM) that encompasses the definition of measurement goals, the definition of metrics, and the interpretation of the measured data in the underlying context.

3 Measuring the Impact of Emergence

The objective of this section is to motivate and outline a goal-oriented approach for quantitatively evaluating the techniques and tools developed in the context of Emergent Software or Emergence technologies in the context of the German Software Cluster research project. This means that the effects of introducing these technologies in industrial settings are measured by conducting empirical studies and then aggregated in order to obtain a more reliable picture of the anticipated effects for upcoming projects and settings.

Subsequently, we will first explain the motivations for quantitative technology evaluation in a research project setting with multiple partners (Sect. 3.1); then we will present the GQM framework for technology evaluation, which gives a simplified view of the key concepts (Sect. 3.2); next, we will summarize the key organizational challenges for quantitative technology evaluation in such settings (Sect. 3.3) and will finally outline GQM-Strategies approach to addressing them (Sect. 3.4).

3.1 Stakeholders and Motivations

The specific reasons motivating technology evaluation depend on the types of stakeholders in focus. In the remainder of this paper, we will list several motivations by distinguishing between three different views on a research project: the view of the technology providers (i.e., research partners and tool vendors), the view of the use case providers (i.e., the industry partners that plan to apply the new technologies in their organization), and the external view (i.e., the funding agencies and companies outside the project that could potentially profit from the project results).

As a *technology provider*, it is important to understand the impact of newly developed techniques and tools on performance in real-world development projects. The sound evaluation of new techniques and tools in different industrial settings can demonstrate their usefulness on the one hand and provide directions for further improvement on the other hand.

As a *use case provider* and potential user of a newly developed technology, it is important to quantitatively assess the potential benefits and costs resulting from the introduction of this technology in one's own development and testing process. Rolling out a new technology without understanding the effects on one's own business objectives and without any sound evaluation in a pilot project (e.g., a case study) would represent an incalculable risk (Lindstrom 1993). Moreover, because a company usually has to spend money when participating in a research project, the benefits of the project have to be explained and demonstrated to higher-level management.

From an *external view*, it is important for a project consortium to demonstrate the success of a project to their national or international sponsors. More and more funding agencies explicitly request that project results shall be quantitatively evaluated to check whether they meet the objectives stated in the project proposal. Moreover, providing sound empirical evaluations will build up confidence in the developed technologies, and thus support their dissemination outside the project: Other researchers and interested companies can learn about the observed method-product relations in order to efficiently adapt and use the developed techniques in new applications and organizations.

3.2 A Framework for Technology Evaluation

In a simplified view, each approach aimed at the quantitative evaluation of technology-based improvements in a given industrial setting has to comprise three groups of key activities, which are briefly introduced below:

1. *Preparing the evaluation of the project objectives*: In order to evaluate the improvement objectives, they have to be operationalized, i.e., we have to define how they are measured and which data need to be collected. An objective can be, for instance, to reduce coding effort by applying a new technology, which may be evaluated by defining (among other things) a measure that quantifies this goal by 'coding effort per Function Point' (CE) in person-hours.
2. *Setting up and conducting empirical studies*: Subsequently, the measures defined in the first step are instantiated by the individual use case providers (UC_i), i.e., they have to set up concrete measurement plans that define how to collect them. During an evaluation phase, they gather the corresponding data for (1) a project, release, or set of modules where the current technology is applied to get a baseline, in our example an effort per Function Point baseline (CE_{B,UC_i}) and for (2) a project, release, or set of modules where the new technology is applied to get the effort per Function Point with the new technology (CE_{NEW,UC_i}). Once both values are available, we can calculate the relative change/improvement resulting from the application of the new technology, in our example the percentage reduction of coding effort ($\%RCE_{U-C\_i} = (CE_{B,UC\_i} - CE_{NEW,UC\_i}) / CE_{B,UC\_i} * 100\ \%$).
3. *Analysis and packaging of results*: Finally, the percentage reductions of coding effort measured in the individual use cases have to be brought together to get a broader picture of the effect of the new technology on coding effort. The individual use-case-specific values are analyzed, aggregated, and reported. In our example, we can calculate, for instance, the average percentage reduction of testing effort: a $\%RCE = 1/n * SUM(\%RCE_{UC\_i=1...n})$. However, depending on the available data, also more advanced analysis can be applied to identify, for instance, factors that are responsible for the variation of results observed in different studies (also referred to as *variation or confounding factors*).

The previously presented activities and short examples are only intended to illustrate the underlying concepts to provide a basic understanding of the major activities. The systematic approach outlined in the following is based on the Goal Question Metric (GQM) and Quality Improvement Paradigm (QIP) (Basili et al. 1994; Basili 1984), a well-known framework for goal-oriented measurement in continuous improvement projects. It consists of six phases, which further refines the three groups of key activities introduced above (Fig. 1).

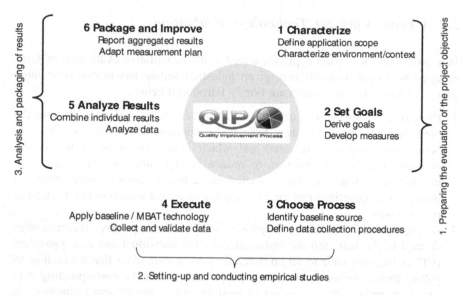

3. Analysis and packaging of results

6 Package and Improve
Report aggregated results
Adapt measurement plan

1 Characterize
Define application scope
Characterize environment/context

5 Analyze Results
Combine individual results
Analyze data

2 Set Goals
Derive goals
Develop measures

1. Preparing the evaluation of the project objectives

4 Execute
Apply baseline / MBAT technology
Collect and validate data

3 Choose Process
Identify baseline source
Define data collection procedures

2. Setting-up and conducting empirical studies

Fig. 1 Evaluating improvements with goal-oriented measurement based on QIP

3.3 Key Challenges

Experience in technology transfer and process improvement projects has shown that one is typically confronted with a set of similar challenges when conducting quantitative technology evaluation. Kläs et al. presented in (2012) the results of a focus group meeting with eleven experts for empirical research. They identified 17 challenges, which were consolidated into four sets: organizational issues, collecting the right data, providing combinable data, and defining a baseline:

1. *Organization issues*: Organizational issues deal with scheduling, distribution of efforts, and empowerment of roles. Unlike the remaining challenges, they are rather independent of the actual approach of technology evaluation, but have to be addressed in the organization and management of considered project.
2. *Collecting the right data*: In practice, the collection of data required to quantify the obtained improvements is often considered a major challenge. The most critical points include that, on the one hand, the measures have to be clearly defined and address the goals of the research project; on the other hand, data collection has to be well motivated for each individual study, especially in research projects where potential study providers cannot be forced to collect data but have to be convinced that they will personally benefit from such data collection.
3. *Providing combinable data*: In order to get more general statements on the effects of new technologies, case-study-specific measurement results have to be provided and combined from several independent studies. In large research

projects, this is usually difficult due to (a) confidentiality issues and (b) the different environments in which these data were collected. Productivity or defect numbers, in particular, are usually considered as very sensitive data that most companies do not want to share. Moreover, such numbers are rarely comparable directly (as they are measured differently in diverse settings) and thus difficult to combine or aggregate.

4. *Defining a baseline*: In order to evaluate improvements resulting from a new technology, we need a starting point for comparison: Although we can *characterize* the performance of a new technology by collecting appropriate measurement data during a case study, we cannot *evaluate* its performance (e.g., show improvements) without a second reference measurement, the baseline. Therefore, in this context the meaning of baseline can be understood as being very similar to its meaning in project management, where a "baseline is the boundary marker from which we can measure progress" (Budd and Budd 2010). As a consequence, identifying a source for collecting appropriate baseline data is one of the most essential tasks in technology evaluation. However, this task is especially difficult in research projects with many case studies since experienced researchers with an empirical background are usually not involved deeply enough in each case study to guide and support baseline data collection. On the other hand, for the people responsible for a case study it is typically not clear where baseline data can be obtained, what the advantages and limitations of the different sources of baseline data are, and how they can deal with confidentiality issues if sensitive company data are involved.

3.4 An Approach for Organizational Alignment of Technology Evaluation

This section outlines an approach for addressing the challenges mentioned in Sect. 3.3. The approach proposes a process for aligning the goals in a research project between various project partners, defining baselines, and deriving individual measurement plans. It was first presented in Kläs (2012) and is based on GQM⁺Strategies® (Basili et al. 2010), the concept of abstract measures, and internal baselines.

In the following, we first briefly introduce the GQM⁺Strategies meta-model, then illustrate how it can be used to model cross-organizational project goals and get them aligned with the organization-specific goals and measurement activities in specific case studies.

3.4.1 Foundations of the GQM⁺Strategies Approach

This section briefly introduces the GQM⁺Strategies® approach based on the summary in (Heidrich et al. to appear). GQM⁺Strategies® (Basili et al. 2010) is a measurement planning and analysis approach that provides a framework and

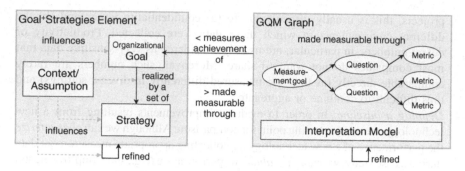

Fig. 2 The GQM⁺strategies® grid meta-model (Heidrich et al. to appear)

notation to help organizations develop/package their operational, measureable business goals, select strategies for implementing them, communicate those goals and strategies throughout the organization, translate those goals into lower-levels goals and strategies down to the level of projects, assess the effectiveness of their strategies at all levels of the organization, and recognize the achievement of their business goals. The output of the GQM⁺Strategies® approach is a detailed and comprehensive model that defines all the elements necessary for a measurement program. GQM⁺Strategies® makes the business goals, strategies, and corresponding lower-level goals explicit.

In the past, a variety of approaches have been developed covering different aspects of linking activities related to IT services and software development to upper-level goals of the organization and demonstrating their business value [such as Balanced Scorecard (Kaplan et al. 1992) and CoBIT® (ISACA 2007)]. The aim of GQM⁺Strategies® is not to replace these approaches, but to close the existing gaps with respect to linking goals, their implementation, and the measurement data needed to evaluate goal attainment.

Figure 2 illustrates the basic concepts of the approach. The left side describes a hierarchy of organizational goals and strategies. Organizational goals define a target state the organization wants to accomplish within a given time frame (e.g., improved customer satisfaction or reduced rework costs). Strategies are possible approaches for achieving a goal within the environment of the organization. Context factors and assumptions give some rationale for the refinement hierarchy. Context factors represent all kinds of factors the organization knows for sure, whereas assumptions are estimated unknowns, i.e., what is believed to be true but needs to be re-evaluated over time.

GQM graphs define how to measure whether a goal was accomplished and whether a strategy was successful. Following the classical Goal/Question/Metric approach (Basili et al. 1994a), goals are broken down into concrete metrics. Interpretation models are used for objectively evaluating goals and strategies.

3.4.2 Identification and Consolidation of General Project Goals

In a first step, according to (Kläs et al. 2012) a set of general overall goals has to be defined based on the objectives of the research project. These objectives can usually be extracted from the project proposal or elicited in a workshop during the starting phase of the project. Examples of typical goals are:

- Reduce rework costs by 30 %;
- Reduce verification and validation costs by 25 %;
- Reduce total cost of ownership for development platform by 10 %;
- Reduce time to market for emergent software systems by 15 %.

However, these goals should be made more concrete with more specific sub-goals and strategies, which should obviously include the application of techniques or tools planned to be developed in the specific research project. This refinement needs to be done jointly by measurement and domain experts since the project proposal or workshop results are usually not detailed enough and contain gaps and ambiguities regarding goals and strategies that need to be resolved. Typical cases are that strategies are mentioned without a clear link to the goal they address or vice versa—that goals are stated without any explanation of how exactly they are to be achieved.

Once an initial version of the refined goal and strategy graphs has been developed, a questionnaire should be used to ask all use case providers to check for completeness, identify dispensable parts, and assure a common understanding throughout the consortium (Kläs et al. 2012). This feedback is then integrated into a consolidated version of the graph. Figure 3 presents an example of such a consolidated goal and strategy graph, which was developed in a research project named MBAT.[2]

3.4.3 Alignment with Organizational Objectives and Quantification

Not each project-related goal has the same relevance in the context of each use case. Moreover, in different use cases, different combinations of strategies (e.g., a selection of specific technologies) can be followed to reach a specific project-related goal. Therefore, use cases will typically not collect measurement data for all, but only for a selection of sub-goals defined in the Goals⁺Strategies graphs.

The GQM⁺Strategies® approach can help an organization to identify the relevant project-related goals and motivate their measurement by aligning them with its own organizational goals. It can achieve this by developing its own use-case-specific Goals+Strategies graphs based on the general Goals+Strategies graphs, which is illustrated in Fig. 4. These customized graphs can then be used by the use

---

2 MBAT project website: www.mbat-artemis.eu.

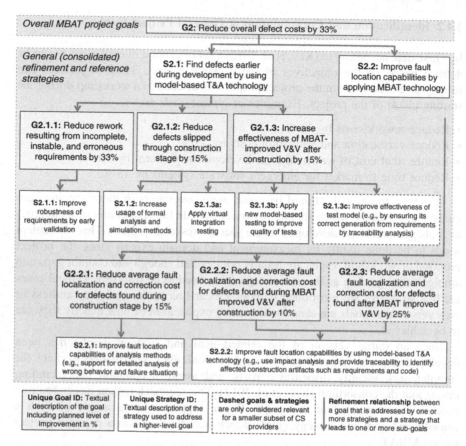

Fig. 3 General refinement of overall project goal G2 in the MBAT project (Kläs et al. 2012)

case providers to show the relevance of specific project-related goals internally and to motivate the collection of data.

In a final step, for each use case, all use-case-relevant goals should be quantified using the Goal/Question/Metric approach (Basili et al. 1994a). The resulting measurement plans aim at supporting the use case provider in concretizing the general project goals and implementing concrete measures and data collection procedures. Moreover, they support the consistent interpretation and aggregation of the collected measurement data after the case studies.

In order to achieve these objectives, a template is proposed in (Kläs et al. 2012) that documents the goal that is to be evaluated and the strategy/strategies implemented in the case study for achieving this goal. Moreover, it asks how the strategy is implemented in the case study through specific methods, tooling, and procedures.

The template also allows documenting the source of baseline data as well as information about the context in which the baseline data are planned to be

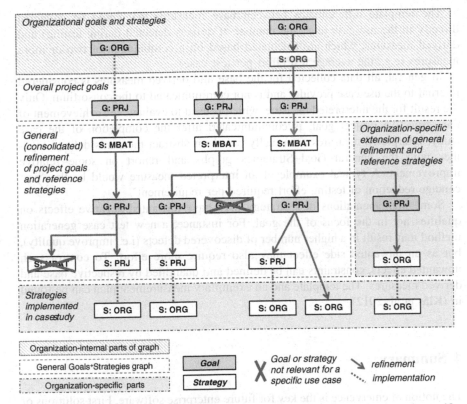

Fig. 4 Relationships between high-level organizational, general project, and case-study-specific goals and strategies based on (Kläs et al. 2012)

collected. More details about different sources of baseline data as well as their advantages and disadvantages are discussed in (Kläs et al. 2012).

In order to derive concrete measures based on the goal, in a first step the measurement goal is documented in a structured way using the Goal/Question/Metric goal template (Basili et al. 1994a). The template separates the purpose of the measurement, the quality aspect in focus (e.g., quality or effort), the object that should be addressed (e.g., an artifact or process), the perspective (viewpoint) from which the measurement goal is defined, and the context in which the measurement is performed and interpreted. Next, relevant measures are derived on the basis of five predefined questions:

- Q1: Which level of improvement was obtained regarding the quality in focus?
- Q2: Which factors differentiate the baseline from the study when the strategies were applied and may influence the results?
- Q3: Was measurement performed correctly when the strategies were applied?
- Q4: Was measurement performed correctly when collecting the baseline data?
- Q5: Were the strategies implemented correctly?

The template differentiates between base measures that could be collected directly in the use case (e.g., the number of defects detected during testing) and derived measures, which are calculated based on a combination of two or more measures (e.g., the average test effort per test case).

In general, all data collected for the base and derived measures is considered internal to the use case provider and is not communicated to the consortium. Only the result for the interpreted measure, which is used to evaluate the achievement of the respective project goal, is communicated after the completion of the case study. Interpreted measures are usually based on abstract measures defined together with the general Goal+Strategies graphs and report on some relative improvement. A typical example of an interpreted measure would be the 'percentage reduction of testing effort required per requirement'.

Some implementations of a strategy may have unwanted negative effects on qualities not in the focus of the goal. For instance, a new test case generation method may result in a higher number of discovered defects (i.e., improve quality), but as an unwanted side effect may also require more effort. To control such unwanted effects, constraints can be defined and quantified by respective base and derived measures. The template and an exemplary measurement plan can be found in (Kläs et al. 2012).

4 Summary

The notion of emergence is the key for future enterprise software. First solutions of emergent technologies and tools are currently implemented in industry-strength software systems and academic prototypes. Now the great challenge lies in measuring the effect of these new concepts and technologies in business software. In this paper, we presented an approach for quantitatively evaluating the techniques and tools developed in the context of Emergent Software. The approach consists of an abstract framework for technology evaluation, which provides a simplified view on the key concepts and a new process for aligning the goals in a research project between various project partners, for defining baselines, and for deriving individual measurement plans. We also presented the GQM+Strategies model and illustrated how it can be used to model cross-organizational project goals and get them aligned with the organization-specific goals and measurement activities in concrete case studies.

Acknowledgments The work presented in this paper was partially funded by the Software-Cluster projects EMERGENT and SINNODIUM (www.software-cluster.org) under grant no. 01IC10S01 and 01IC12S01F, the ARTEMIS Joint Undertaking under grant agreement no. 269335, and the German Federal Ministry of Education and Research (BMBF). The authors assume responsibility for the content.

References

Basili VR (1984) Quantitative evaluation of software engineering methodology. In: Proceedings of 1st Pan Pacific computer conference, 1984b

Basili VR, Caldiera G, Rombach HD (1994a) The experience factory. In: Marciniak JJ (ed) Encyclopedia software engineering, vol 1. Wiley, New York, pp 469–476

Basili VR, Caldiera G, Rombach HD (1994b) Goal, question, metric paradigm. In: Marciniak JJ (ed) Encyclopedia of software engineering, vol 1. Wiley, New York, pp 528–532

Basili V et al (2010) Linking software development and business strategy through measurement. Computer 2010(43):57–65

Budd CI, Budd CS (2010) A practical guide to earned value project management. Management Concepts, VA

Frischbier S, Gesmann M, Mayer D, Roth A, Webel C (2012) Emergence as competitive advantage-engineering tomorrow's enterprise software systems. In: Proceedings of the 14th international conference on enterprise information systems (ICEIS 2012), Wroclaw, Poland, ISBN 978-989-8565-12-9, July 2012

Heidrich J, Rombach D, Kläs M (2014) Model-based Quality Management of Software Development Projects. In: Ruhe G, Wohlin C (eds) Software project management in a changing world, Springer

ISACA (2007) Control objectives for information and related technology (CoBIT®). Retrieved 04/ Dec /2007, from www.isaca.org

Kaplan R, Norton D (1992) The balanced scorecard—measures that drive performance. Harvard Business Review, Massachusetts Jan–Feb 1992, p 71

Kläs M, Bauer T, Tiberi U (2012) Beyond herding cats: aligning quantitative technology evaluation in large-scale research projects. In: Proceedings of 14th international conference on product-focused software development and process improvement (PROFES 2012). Paphos, Cyprus, 2012

Lindstrom D (1993) Five ways to destroy a development project. Softw, IEEE. 1993(10):55–58

Information Systems Integration in the Cloud: Scenarios, Challenges and Technology Trends

Michael Kleeberg, Christian Zirpins and Holger Kirchner

Abstract Modern enterprise-IT-landscapes increasingly include best-of-breed business applications, platforms and infrastructure sourced on demand from cloud service providers. Such IT-cloud-sourcing fosters both scalability and flexibility of enterprise information systems, which enables fast responses to ever-changing market needs and competition. However, cloud computing also extends the need for and range of information systems integration: mixed cloud-/on-premise-IT-landscapes extend integration of data, components and processes beyond the boundaries of a single enterprise combining them with B2B integration and cross-enterprise collaboration. Furthermore, integration technology providers increasingly offer their solutions as-a-service in the cloud, which also allows them to extend their portfolios in response to technology trends like big data or mobile outreach. In this paper we analyze current practices and upcoming trends of information systems integration in the context of cloud computing technology. This includes a discussion of cloud integration scenarios and related challenges from multiple perspectives. Subsequently, we draw a vision of a cloud-based integration technology stack that enables a wide range of federated cloud integration solutions.

M. Kleeberg (✉) · C. Zirpins · H. Kirchner
Seeburger Ag, Edisonstr. 1, 75015 Bretten, Germany
e-mail: m.kleeberg@seeburger.de

C. Zirpins
e-mail: c.zirpins@seeburger.de

H. Kirchner
e-mail: h.kirchner@seeburger.de

G. Brunetti et al. (eds.), *Future Business Software*,
Progress in IS, DOI: 10.1007/978-3-319-04144-5_4,
© Springer International Publishing Switzerland 2014

1 Introduction

Today, enterprises face constant pressure to meet the always changing challenges of competition on globalized markets. Their ability to stay competitive, responsive and flexible as well as to collaborate in business networks on global scale is vitally based on ICT as the enabling factor and translates into a variety of requirements for *enterprise information systems* (Da Xu 2011).

Enterprise information systems are expected to implement business processes in a flexible and agile yet ergonomic way and provide visibility and fast delivery on a global scale. These abilities should go along with high availability, scalability and security as well as guaranteed process/data compliance. Finally, there is a demand for pay-per-use and on-demand sourcing for lowering operating costs and speeding up return on investment.

In this context, capabilities of enterprise information systems to *integrate* in diverse ways, within and beyond organizational boundaries, get more important than ever. Increasingly, *information systems integration* has to reach beyond the classical aspects of interconnecting data, applications and processes within enterprise application landscapes or business-to-business transactions. In terms of capabilities, modern integration technology has to consider large scale enterprise information (aka big data), a plethora of mobile devices and sensors as well as the complex networks introduced by social communities. Even more fundamental, information system integration is faced with the rise of cloud computing, which has led to radical changes in the sourcing of enterprise IT.

The paradigm of *cloud computing* promotes dynamic provisioning and on-demand consumption of virtualized-resources as electronic service via computer networks like the Internet (Armbrust et al. 2010). The main classes of cloud offerings include Infrastructure- (IaaS), Platforms- (PaaS) and Software-as-a-Service (SaaS). The underlying rationale is a striking win–win situation: Cloud providers increase resource utilization while leveraging economies of scale. Cloud consumers gain the ability to scale on-demand (aka elasticity) while paying on a per-use basis.

Cloud computing extends the information system landscape of single enterprises beyond their physical and organizational boundaries, because data, applications and processes might be hosted or provided by third party providers. However, common intra-enterprise integration platforms and services have not been designed to cope with the problems of leaving the context of a single enterprise. Moreover, novel business-to-business transactions are needed between cloud consumers and providers.

In contrast, integration platforms and services might be provided from the cloud themselves. This offers opportunities for substantial gains in diversity, manageability and scalability of integration capabilities. This opportunity is seen by many as a possible answer to the current challenges of information systems integration.

In this paper we shed light on scenarios of and challenges for information systems integration that are being introduced by cloud computing today. We will also discuss, how cloud computing might be leveraged by integration technology to cope with current challenges of integration diversity. Consequently, we propose an architectural stack for cloud-enabled integration technology that enables a broad diversity of federated integration solutions. Overall, our contribution is a broad vision for cloud-enabled information systems integration.

The rest of the paper is structured as follows: Sect. 2 starts with an outline of the state-of-the-art in information system integration. In contrast to that, Sect. 3 introduces novel scenarios of integration in the context of cloud computing. Consequently, Sect. 4 discusses related challenges from different perspectives and Sect. 5 derives vital features of cloud-enabled integration platform- and service-technologies. Finally, Sect. 6 discusses related work and Sect. 7 concludes.

2 State-of-the-Art in Information Systems Integration

Integration of business applications (or more generally *information systems*), whether within (A2A) or across (B2B) enterprise borders, can be generally divided into the following three tasks (Kurz et al. 2001):

- *Data integration* aims at maintaining consistency of logical data units shared by multiple information systems within a variety of heterogeneous data stores.
- *Application integration* provides means to compose complex functionality from multiple discrete application components into a coherent aggregate.
- *Business process integration* maps business activities of a managed multistep process into data transformation for and communication with discrete system parts.

Due to business requirements, respective integration solutions are usually required to provide end-to-end security, monitoring/auditing/tracking facilities, means to ensure high availability, and complex business process management (BPM) support (Kurz et al. 2001).

Common *integration platforms and services* provide reliable, scalable, and highly available means to implement integration solutions. They totally secure and constantly track integrative business transactions, whether these are being processed, in-motion or in-rest. Business processes might be long running and multilateral.

Integration solutions are frequently classified by their focus on *inter-* or *intra-enterprise integration*. These classes will be further detailed in the following.

2.1 Intra-Enterprise Integration and EAI Technology

The need for intra-enterprise integration often arises from the existence of isolated data and application silos within different organizational units. Respective enterprise application integration (EAI) aims to bridge these silos in order to reduce processing times and efforts of the individual applications, to increase data quality, and to realize cost savings due to a higher degree of automation.

Traditionally, enterprise internal business processes (also called *private processes*) have been implicitly realized within individual business applications or explicitly targeted by workflow systems. In contrast, most inter-enterprise integration solutions have a focus on data- and application integration tasks.

From an architectural perspective, EAI-solutions provide support on the communication-, data-, application- and presentation layer (He and Xu 2012). This includes

- a wide range of standard-based *communication protocols* (e.g. IIOP[1] or HTTP[2]),
- *mapping and transformation facilities* for data schemas and formats (e.g. XSLT[3]),
- *middleware* for interoperable interaction of software components [e.g. via RPC, ORB or MOM (Bishop and Karne 2003)] and managed *runtime containers* (e.g. J2EE,[4].NET[5]) and
- *UI integration technologies* like portal frameworks or mashup environments (Minsk et al. 2007).

The increasing heterogeneity of EAI-technologies has led to efforts aiming at middleware interoperability by means of common Internet technologies (He and Da Xu 2012). This has resulted in Web Services and the WS*-architecture stack of XML-based protocols (Issarny et al. 2011). Many EAI platforms provide holistic service-oriented approaches, structuring application landscapes in Service-Oriented Architecture (SOA) integrated by Enterprise Service Bus (ESB) infrastructure. Moreover, such technologies are increasingly leveraged for inter-enterprise integration, as described in the next Sect. 2.2.

2.2 Inter-Enterprise Integration and B2Bi Technology

Inter-enterprise integration is predominantly motivated by the need for agile and flexible realization of so called *business-to-business (B2B)* applications running an increasing amount of inter-organizational business transactions, e.g. in the context of supply-chains or other forms of collaborative business networks.

---

[1] http://www.corba.org/

[2] http://tools.ietf.org/html/rfc2616

[3] http://www.w3.org/TR/xslt20/

[4] http://www.oracle.com/technetwork/java/javaee/overview/index.html

[5] http://msdn.microsoft.com/de-de/vstudio/aa496123

Automated B2B-transactions might lead to reduced inventories, processing costs, procurement planning risks, and throughput times, while promising better data quality, improved customer retention, and general cost savings.

Business application interoperability fundamentally builds upon the three layers of *communication*, *business processes*, and *documents* (Kabak and Dogac 2010). Respective *B2B-integration (B2Bi)* platforms and services mostly focus on the processes and protocols underlying external business transactions (also called *public processes*).

Because B2B-transactions leave the context of one trusted and controlled environment, B2Bi technologies provide high levels of reliability, availability, robustness, failure-tolerance, traceability, and security. Document and protocol types need to be agreed upon by all involved parties.

A large variety of national and international standards (e.g. EDIFACT,[6] ebXML,[7] RosettaNet[8]) has been established for B2B-applications, including secure communication protocols (e.g. X.400,[9] OFTP[10]), common message and document formats to exchange [e.g. UBL, BODs, GS1 (Kabak and Dogac 2010)], as well as public processes and protocols to follow [e.g. BPEL, BPSS, PIPs (Jung et al. 2006)].

Furthermore, reference models have been developed (e.g. SCOR[11]) that provide common understanding, methodology and terminology of business systems integration between disparate enterprises (Hvolby and Trienekens 2010). All such standards might be generic or relate to specific industries/use cases.

3 Integration Scenarios in the Cloud

The advent of cloud computing has led to substantial changes in the way that enterprises make use of and operate ICT. These changes are also affecting information systems integration. In particular, integration technology providers need to rethink what is being integrated where and how the integration needs to be done accordingly.

A variety of integration scenarios can be envisaged in various cloud setups. To ease the discussion, we classify these scenarios across three dimensions:

- **by cloud service type**: cloud services might be resources to be integrated or on-demand integration technologies:

---

6 http://www.unece.org/cefact/edifact/welcome.html

7 http://www.ebxml.org/

8 http://www.rosettanet.org/

9 http://www.itu.int/rec/T-REC-X.400/en

10 http://www.ietf.org/rfc/rfc5024

11 http://supply-chain.org/

- *Cloud Service Integration* means techniques for the integration of cloud services like data stored within IaaS, software components hosted in a PaaS or SaaS applications providing APIs.
- *Cloud Integration Services* are integration technologies (platforms or services) provided as cloud services. Cloud integration services are also known as *Integration-as-a-Service (IaaS)* or *Integration-Platform-as-a-Service (iPaaS)* (Pezzini and Lheureux 2011).

- **by cloud topology**: integration might involve systems that are hosted in any combination of cloud and on-premise environments:

  - In situations of *cloud-to-cloud* integration, all integrated systems are given as services hosted in a cloud environment, which might be *homogeneous* (one cloud provider) or *heterogeneous* (multiple cloud providers).
  - The case of *cloud-to-on-premise* integration involves legacy information systems in the enterprise that are being integrated with data or applications that are provided as cloud services.
  - *On-premise-to-on-premise* integration solely involves information systems that are hosted on-premise. These systems are being integrated by means of cloud integration services.

- **by integration type**: integration might relate to EAI or B2Bi scenarios:

  - Scenarios of *EAI-in-the-Cloud* aim to integrate information systems within the logical boundaries of and for the sole use within a single enterprise. This might involve cloud integration services (e.g. virtualized message queues like Amazon SQS[12]) and/or cloud services integration (e.g. data stores as IaaS).
  - The goal of *B2Bi-in-the-cloud* is to support B2B-transactions between groups of collaborating enterprises. Again, this might involve cloud integration services (e.g. B2B-hubs as iPaaS) and/or cloud services integration (e.g. enterprises hosting their messaging endpoints in the cloud).

The broad spectrum of possible scenarios ranges from cases that are already commonplace to others that are still rather visionary. A common integration scenario in the cloud is given by *B2B Integration Services*: Many vendors are offering on-premise-to-on-premise B2B solutions as services via private or public cloud environments.

B2B integration services might be generic (e.g. data exchange services[13] like managed file transfer) or industry-specific (e.g. running standard processes in the utilities industry[14]). Enterprises can benefit from on-demand usage of state-of-the-art solutions without taking high risks as such services are mostly based on rather mature IaaS, PaaS or SaaS technologies.

---

[12] http://aws.amazon.com/sqs/

[13] http://www.seeburger.eu/standard-cloud-services/collaboration-cloud/exchange.html

[14] http://www.seeburger.eu/standard-cloud-services/wim-cloud-services.html

Today, many enterprises have already outsourced parts of their information systems landscape to the cloud and need to integrate these with their legacy systems. We refer to this common use case as *cloud-to-on-premise-EAI*. For example, many enterprises are using salesforce.com CRM-SaaS solutions[15] (e.g. Sales Cloud or Service Cloud) and frequently require synchronizing master data with on-premise ERP-solutions (e.g. SAP). A respective integration solution requires bidirectional master data synchronization with tight time constraints over public networks.

In many cases, such solutions can be based upon extensions of common EAI technology, considering the technical conditions of specific cloud providers (e.g. in the above example, an integration solution would need to consider salesforce.com APIs and force.com PaaS technology). However, additional challenges emerge from leaving the organizational and technical boundaries of the enterprise, including security, robustness, and performance issues.

Some more visionary scenarios can be found in the area of *cloud-to-cloud-EAI*, which offers unique opportunities to cope with novel integration challenges. Some major trends requiring novel integration solutions, including big data analytics, end-user interaction via mobile devices, community-driven commerce, and cyber-physical systems are themselves heavily based on cloud computing techniques.

For example, in mobile-to-mobile applications (M2M) massive data streams, as produced by large sensor/device networks, are increasingly utilized to provide value-added services. If both sensor data storage and service processing are based on cloud infrastructure, sophisticated integration technology is required, which itself might be hosted in the cloud (see Axeda[16] for example).

Clearly, cloud-to-cloud-EAI shows characteristics that are different from traditional EAI integration scenarios. Beyond the off-premise burden, these are for instance related to extremely large scales of data and connection volumes. A variety of specific integration solutions can be expected to emerge from this field.

EAI-in-the-cloud leads to a situation, where more enterprise resources are being exposed to off-premise access or moved to the cloud. This situation opens novel opportunities for supporting B2B-transactions. In such scenarios (referred to as *B2Bi-via-EAI-in-the-cloud*), integration technologies with a traditional focus on EAI are used to interconnect information systems of collaborating enterprises.

A straight forward example is cross-enterprise data sharing by means of a common cloud-based data store. This kind of sharing is often a goal for closely related organizations, e.g. savings banks sharing client master data with their investment- or insurance subsidiaries. This kind of integration is particularly challenging as the high quality-levels required for B2Bi-solutions need to be achieved for mostly finer grained EAI-techniques. Moreover, the usage of cloud integration services requires additional B2B-transactions to be established with cloud service providers.

---

[15] http://www.salesforce.com/
[16] http://www.axeda.com/

Novel scenarios of information system integration usage, as discussed so far, go along with novel scenarios of integration technology provisioning. Some of the scenarios lead to requirements that cross the traditional classes of integration technology or extend them. For complex cases, few integration technology providers will be willing or able to offer an adequate portfolio of integration services. *Federated cloud integration services* might be an answer to this problem.

Federated cloud integration services comprise complementing technologies (EAI/B2Bi/special purpose integration) that together fulfill the requirements of complex cloud integration scenarios. Respective integration services share common models and federation platform services, enabling the combination of different providers into a holistic solution.

It is obvious that the full potential of cloud based integration scenarios is not tapped today. In particular we claim that the more challenging scenarios of cloud-to-cloud EAI, B2Bi-via-EAI-in-the-cloud, and federated cloud integration services are not appropriately supported by common integration solutions today. In the next section, we will outline the major challenges that need to be addressed.

4 Challenges for Cloud Integration

Concerning the integration scenarios described above, a wide spectrum of challenges can be identified. These challenges include those faced by both providers of cloud integration platforms, technologies or products, and user organizations that are about to adopt these technologies.

Fundamentally, a couple of technical challenges have to be mastered. However, more challenges emerge in non-technical areas like service market fluctuation, organizational issues, and questions of economics. More concrete, the following factors can be identified:

- **Technical challenges** relating to technologies that are missing so far:
  - Cloud integration platforms and services need to support *fundamental cloud computing capabilities* like multi-tenancy and elastic scalability. Respective solutions need to handle high workloads while keeping up qualitative characteristics as not to violate SLA guarantees. Depending on skills, resources, and technical characteristics of their product portfolio, integration technology providers might be faced with considerable R&D challenges.
  - *Basic security and privacy* are still a major challenge in cloud integration, especially concerning the usually required existence of trusted parties. Novel cryptographic technologies are promising to alleviate this situation.
  - Partly related to missing cloud computing standards, cloud integration technology might be faced with problems of *connectivity and interoperability of cloud services*. For example, SaaS-offers don't always include APIs or require proprietary PaaS to be used for external interaction.

- The co-existence of legacy and cloud-based integration technologies might require *technical federation*, including aspects like interoperability, synchronization etc.
- **Market challenges** relating to competing cloud integration providers:
  - User organizations are faced with a high *fragmentation of cloud integration services* offering non-consolidated solutions. This leaves them with challenges like migration between and/or federation of co-existing technologies.
  - In a proprietary world of integration services, significant engagements of user organizations in cloud integration might lead to risky provider dependencies. This situation is generally known in cloud computing as *vendor lock-in*.
  - User organizations in particular are faced with *immature service providers* and therefore need to consider unstable business models and pricing.
  - Providers face a *lack of cloud integration standards* to position their offers and leverage common frameworks, including holistic monitoring, management, and governance structures.
- **Organizational challenges** concerning business management and operation:
  - Both user organizations and providers have to cope with *missing knowledge and industrial best practices*. While users need to acquire skills for leveraging cloud integration services, providers need to familiarize with cloud business models and related processes.
  - A *lack of trust relationships* between users and providers can be prohibitive even with capable security/privacy technologies in place: Tight dependencies might turn out disastrous, e.g. in case of SLA violations in business-critical situations. More general, trust requirements, with respect to partners as well as the technology as such, need to be aligned with organizational strategy and culture.
  - Information systems integration requires support for *governance* of holistic integration solutions as well as *compliance* of relevant parts (e.g. related to legislative constraints). However, respective traditional solutions might be specific and generic solutions need to be found that can be used in a cloud set up.
  - User organizations require *transparency and accountability* of interactions within integration solutions, e.g. in order to prevent data leakage. This requires generic concepts and respective services to be part of cloud integration platforms.
  - The co-existence of legacy and cloud-based integration solutions might require *organizational federation* including governance, life cycle management etc.
- **Economic challenges** relating to financial risks, benefits and trade-offs:
  - A key question for user organizations is about assessing *return on investments*. However, calculation models for long term cumulative costs are scarce and even worse for quantification of potential benefits. In contrast, cloud integration providers need *pricing models* in order to calculate their service offers.

– From a more holistic perspective, both user organizations and providers would greatly benefit from a risk assessment framework allowing them to quantify the consequences of trade-offs with respect to technical, organizational, and economic decisions related to cloud integration solutions.

It has to be mentioned that not all enterprises will face the challenges in the same way and to the same extent because of differences in skills and resources as well as differences between industries.

5 Cloud Integration Technology

Novel technologies are required to support upcoming cloud integration scenarios and address their specific challenges. It is commonly agreed that such technologies will be best provided in a consolidated approach by means of a specialized form of cloud-based platform services referred to as integration platform as a service (iPaaS).

A first characterization is provided by Gartner, defining iPaaS as *"a suite of cloud services enabling development, execution and governance of integration flows connecting any combination of on premises and cloud-based processes, services, applications and data within individual, or across multiple, organizations"* (Pezzini and Lheureux 2011).

In the following, we will discuss the approach in more detail, structuring its presentation into three parts related to distinct technical aspects:

1. *Fundamental Integration Features* enabling the development, operation, management, and governance of solutions for cloud integration scenarios,
2. *Cloud Enabling Features* supporting the virtualization, elastic scaling, and isolated execution of fundamental integration features as services in the cloud and
3. *Service Federation Features* facilitating the collaboration of cloud integration providers to jointly empower integration solutions within a dynamic ecosystem.

Fundamental integration features as well as cloud enabling features are commonly agreed upon in the current literature [see e.g. (Pezzini and Lheureux 2011; Hai and Sakoda 2009; Wlodarczyk et al. 2009; Sun et al. 2007; Potocnik and Juric 2012)], although there are some differences in terms of specific feature sets, their extent, and their structuring. Beyond these, we argue that service federation features are an additional class of capabilities that are not sufficiently addressed so far.

Figure 1 outlines the complete technology stack of cloud integration. In the following sections, we will explain all of its parts in detail.

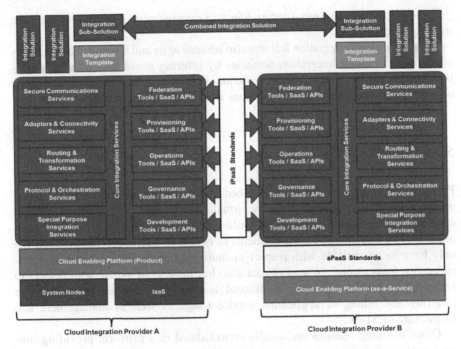

Fig. 1 Generic cloud integration platform architecture

5.1 Fundamental Integration Features

Any integration solution builds on common *core integration features* that reflect the state-of-the-art in EAI and B2Bi. Such core features are well understood and typically include communication channels with end-to-end security, adapters for common legacy systems, standard-compliant messaging and routing, data mapping and transformation, runtime containers for custom integration services, as well as protocol execution and orchestration engines. Beyond common integration solutions, a variety of more specific needs like device connectivity, high-volume/high-frequency data exchange, data flow analytics, complex event processing, or real time processing will be addressed by special purpose integration features.

While core integration features provide an infrastructure for integration solutions, additional features relate to their development, operation and governance. *Development features* include integrated modeling, development, and testing tools. *Operations features* include systems administration, management, and monitoring. Also, consolidated integration technology has to include *governance features* like repositories, lifecycle management, policy tools, message tracking, and auditing.

Typically, cloud integration features also address agile and flexible characteristics often found in cloud integration scenarios by offering *provisioning features* supporting the setup of cloud integration solutions between partners. This might include offering pre-packaged integration solutions as well as self-service capabilities.

5.2 Cloud Enabling Features

Fundamental integration features described so far need to be extended with cloud enabling features to provide them as virtualized services. Fundamentally, cloud enabling features include support for multi-tenant applications that might be used in parallel by a scalable number of clients in isolation. Moreover, applications not only have to be scalable with respect to multiple dimensions (number of users, endpoints, transactions, volume of data etc.) but have to be elastic with respect to variations in demand as well. Additional features are required to support the metering and billing of application service usage as well as management and monitoring of SLAs.

Cloud enabling features are usually consolidated in a platform providing runtime containers and services for generic applications that are to be virtualized and provided on-demand and as-a-service over a network. Such platforms might themselves be packaged as cloud enabled application platform (CEAP) products or application Platform-as-a-Service (aPaaS) via the cloud (Pezzini and Lheureux 2011).

Moreover, iPaaS providers will also need to deploy their complete platform (in the case of using a CEAP-product) or parts of it (when using aPaaS, at least the non-cloud-provided fundamental integration features), either on-premise or again in the cloud, utilizing IaaS. Thus, an iPaaS might in itself vary between a single provider setup or a complex ecosystem also involving multiple providers of aPaaS and IaaS.

5.3 Service Federation Features

Reflecting the range of cloud integration scenarios, the requirements for cloud integration technology will vary widely. While cloud integration technology certainly benefits from consolidation within platforms, it is hardly feasible to develop or seek a single iPaaS-offering to deliver integration solutions for all scenarios. An exhaustive iPaaS would be highly complex and rarely necessary. This is especially true with respect to special purpose integration features.

For the above reasons, an iPaaS should provide modularity, even beyond the scope of a single integration provider. User organizations should be free to choose from and adjust between complementing solutions of different providers in order to realize the full range of their cloud integration scenarios. Moreover, it should even be possible to compose sub-solutions into a holistic solution. This, however, requires features to federate the cloud integration services of multiple cloud integration service providers.

An extreme solution to iPaaS federation would be to introduce just another level of integration (between their proprietary platform services). This would however lead to a substantial increase of complexity compromising potential benefits.

One aspect of a possible solution might be the introduction of *iPaaS-standards*. If certain conceptual models, processes, and APIs would be adhered to by a group of iPaaS providers, the effort of integrating their services could be greatly reduced. This might include standards for a subset of fundamental integration features, which is already true for many B2Bi and EAI features and would be particularly useful in the area of operations management and governance. Additional standards on lower levels like aPaaS or IaaS would further enhance the flexibility of iPaaS providers and potently show through up to the iPaaS level.

6 Related Work

Cloud-based integration services can be found in the portfolio of commercial products offered by many integration technology providers. However, only a few of them include consolidated platforms in the cloud. An overview of the industry players can be found in a Gartner Report on iPaaS (Pezzini and Lheureux 2011). A more detailed market survey is beyond the scope of this paper.

Topics that are directly or indirectly relevant for cloud integration are subject of a variety of research programs, some of which will be mentioned here.

Within the *Theseus* program, which had its focus on the Internet of Services, the project *B2B-in-the-Cloud*[17] has examined self-service capabilities for B2Bi platforms.

The *Trusted-Cloud* program[18] focuses on security and privacy concerns of cloud computing in general and of specific applications in particular. Within Trusted Cloud, the project *Peer Energy Cloud (PEC)*[19] aims, among other things, at cloud integration scenarios in the area of data integration for localized smart power grids and value added services.

The *Software Cluster*[20] targets highly versatile cross-enterprise information system landscapes that show emergent behavior. As a base technology, the

---

[17] http://www.joint-research.org/theseus-mittelstandsprojekte/b2b-in-the-cloud/
[18] http://www.trusted-cloud.de/
[19] http://www.peerenergycloud.de/
[20] http://www.software-cluster.com/en/

program also targets cloud integration aspects, e.g. in its joint projects *EMER-GENT* and *InDiNet*.

The challenges of cloud integration have also started to receive attention from individual research. In the following, we discuss a selection of related results.

The utilization of cloud computing in the context of ERP-systems has been studied by Schubert and Adisa (2011). They point out possibilities for utilizing different cloud computing layers for ERP-related services and emphasize challenges as well as potentials for integration with on-premise legacy applications and business partners.

Wlodarczyk et al. (2009) have examined integration-specific cloud topologies and services with an intra-enterprise focus (referred to as "Enterprise Clouds") and with inter-enterprise scope (referred to as "Industrial Clouds"). In particular, they propose a holistic concept of industrial clouds empowering dynamic collaborative networks.

Cloud-based B2Bi-services have been studied by Bolloju and Murugesan (2012), especially from the perspective of small and medium size enterprises (SMEs). They find that data integration, managed file transfer, and process integration are most relevant to these businesses.

Zhu et al. (2010) have proposed the "SaaSify"-approach, leveraging SaaS to consolidate variants of information systems and thus avoid the need for their integration.

Sun et al. (2010) have explored various design aspects of SaaS, including requirements for integration as part of functional SaaS product design . They have found that especially CRM, F&A, PLM, Inventory, and Procurement SaaS require integration.

Specific problems of integrating SaaS have also been discussed by Sun et al. (2007). This includes data, process, and UI-integration under consideration of security, billing, and SLA-management. They propose a model-driven approach for SaaS-integration based on a SaaS description language (SaaS-DL) and the SaaS integration accelerator (SaaSia) framework supporting multiple deployment modes. Consequently, Potocnik et al. have proposed iPaaS as a strategy to overcome SaaS integration challenges (Potocnik and Juric 2012).

A comprehensive discussion of SaaS integration best practices has been presented by Hai and Sakoda (2009). They set SaaS integration into the EAI context and describe characteristic patterns, including aspects like big data volume and extended governance, based on technologies like Web services, CRUD, and mashups possibly provided as-a-service.

7 Conclusion

Modern enterprises, and especially SMEs, are continuously required to engage in new cross-enterprise business relationships with fast paces and a high frequency of change. Usually, this goes along with the need to integrate their enterprise information systems. Thus, respective integration technologies are required to solve ever changing integration problems. Moreover, these integration problems are getting increasingly complex and more specialized, e.g. with respect to large data volumes being shared and processed, real time devices, mobile outreach, and cloud computing. Due to the required knowledge and resources, it is not always feasible or even possible for enterprises to obtain and continuously extend and adapt respective integration technologies themselves.

Cloud integration technology provides user organizations with integration services and pre-packaged solutions on-demand. Integration technology providers are increasingly offering holistic integration platform services that provide a consolidated set of scalable features, ranging from basic to special purpose integration and governance together with respective means of development and management. Ideally, federation features and standardization will even enable the collaboration of integration technology providers to combine their complementary services. Such combination of cloud based integration technologies opens up an unprecedented range of possible integration solutions.

Consequently, cloud-based integration technology doesn't only help to solve the current problems of integration faced by virtually any modern enterprise, but introduces novel opportunities to them. In particular, an extended range of possible integration solutions enables the emergence of novel enterprise information systems. Respective *emergent information systems* are again driving innovative business- and collaboration models. Thus, cloud integration clearly offers the potential to advance business and provide visionary enterprises with a competitive edge.

References

Armbrust M, Fox A, Griffith R, Joseph AD, Katz R, Konwinski A, Lee G, Patterson D, Rabkin A, Stoica I, Zaharia M (2010) A view of cloud computing. Commun ACM 53:50–58

Bishop T, Karne R (2003) A survey of middleware. In: Debnath NC (ed) Proceedings of the ISCA 18th international conference computers and their applications, Honolulu, Hawaii, USA, ISCA (2003), 26–28 Mar 2003. pp 254–258

Bolloju N, Murugesan S (2012) Cloud-based B2B systems integration for small-and-medium-sized enterprises. In: Proceedings of the international conference on advances in computing, communications and informatics—ICACCI'12, p 477

Da Xu L (2011) Enterprise systems: state-of-the-art and future trends. Ind Inf IEEE Trans 7:630–640

Hai H, Sakoda S (2009) SaaS and integration best practices. Fujitsu Sci Tech J 45:257–264

He W, Xu Da L (2012) Integration of distributed enterprise applications: a survey. IEEE Trans Ind Inf 1

Hvolby H–H, Trienekens JH (2010) Challenges in business systems integration. Comput Ind 61:808–812

Issarny V, Georgantas N, Hachem S, Zarras A, Vassiliadist P, Autili M, Gerosa MA, Hamida AB (2011) Service-oriented middleware for the future internet: state of the art and research directions. J Internet Serv Appl 2:23–45

Jung J-Y, Kim H, Kang S-H (2006) Standards-based approaches to B2B workflow integration. Comput Ind Eng 51:321–334

Kabak Y, Dogac A (2010) A survey and analysis of electronic business document standards. ACM Comput Surv 42:1–31

Kurz C, Hotop E, Haring G (2001) Evaluation and characterization of business-to-business integration systems. In: 4th international conference on electronic commerce research, pp 424–438

Minsk C, Poh S, Siew P (2007) Web 2.0 concepts and technologies for dynamic B2B integration. In: 2007 IEEE conference on emerging technologies & factory automation (EFTA 2007), pp 315–321

Pezzini M, Lheureux B (2011) Integration platform as a service: moving integration to the cloud. Gartner

Potocnik M, Juric MB (2012) Integration of SaaS using IPaaS. In: Trobec R (ed) Proceedings of the 1th international conference on cloud assisted services (CLASS), pp 35–41. Univerza v Ljubljani, Fakulteta za gradbeništvo in geodezijo, Ljubljana (2012)

Schubert P, Adisa F (2011) Cloud computing for standard erp systems: reference framework and research agenda. Arbeitsberichte aus dem Fachbereich Informatik

Sun W, Zhang K, Chen S-K, Zhang X, Liang H (2007) Software as a service: an integration perspective. In: Krämer B, Lin K-J, Narasimhan P (eds) Service-oriented computing—ICSOC 2007. Springer, Berlin, pp 558–569

Sun W, Guo C, Jiang Z, Zhang X, Duan N, Huang Y, Xiong Da Y (2010) Design aspects of software as a service to enable e-business through cloud platform. In: 2010 IEEE 7th international conference on e-business engineering, pp 456–461

Wlodarczyk T, Rong C, Thorsen K (2009) Industrial cloud: toward inter-enterprise integration. In: Proceeding cloudCom'09 the 1st international conference on cloud computing, pp 460–471

Zhu Z, Chen L, Song J, Liu G (2010) Applying SaaS architecture to large enterprises for enterprise application integration. In: 2nd international conference on information science and engineering (ICISE), IEEE 2010, pp 1887–1890

Process on Demand: Planning and Control of Adaptive Business Processes

Thomas Feld and Michael Hoffmann

1 Introduction

Today, managers are facing a fast-moving business environment with changing customer needs and expectations, fast-evolving technologies and product lifecycles, strong globalization effects, accelerating innovation, and increasing digitization of products. Within this environment, managers need to ensure long-term business success for their company. In a growing market, it is important to respond by investing in innovative new products, sales channels, and marketing strategies. Organizations operating in a tough economic environment, on the other hand, need to focus on optimizing costs, timescales, and product resources in order to boost efficiency.

Long-term business success is all about the ability of an organization to respond quickly to the changing market conditions, adapting their business model, and bringing their market strategy to operational execution through appropriate business processes, people, and technologies.

Business Process Management (BPM) is essential to ensure long-term business success based on flexible, market-responsive structures that simultaneously promote efficiency.

The challenge is the management of individualized process variants. If we think of the discussion about the 4th industrial revolution, where the average production batch decreases to one product per order, an infinite volume of process variants is predetermined.

T. Feld (✉)
Vice President for Research and Innovation, Scheer Group: The Innovation Network,
Saarbrücken, Germany
e-mail: thomas.feld@scheer-group.com

M. Hoffmann
Research and Solution Management, Scheer Management GmbH Consulting and Solutions,
Saarbrücken, Germany
e-mail: michael.hoffmann@scheer-management.com

G. Brunetti et al. (eds.), *Future Business Software*,
Progress in IS, DOI: 10.1007/978-3-319-04144-5_5,
© Springer International Publishing Switzerland 2014

Section 2 gives a short overview of existing megatrends that require flexible adoption of business processes. Section 3 introduces an extended methodology for business process management (BPM) and the implementation of business processes that enables a flexible and rapid adoption. Section 4 describes an exemplary implementation at the research project InDiNet and shows the realization of a software service that supports an external help desk as a service. Section 5 gives an outlook to the future.

2 Megatrends

Megatrends reflect change processes that span decades. Indeed, trends have intensified and picked up speed, especially in the IT-industry (Fig. 1).

2.1 Social Collaboration

Social Collaboration means to combine two principles of cooperative work. The first is to share thoughts and problems of actual working situation with other people like employees, customers or suppliers. The second principle is the personal responsibility for products, solutions or results. Via social networks, diversity of opinion and the wisdom of crowds can be used to get faster or even better results in daily work.

2.2 Mass Customization

Every one wants to be unique. So we all prefer things that have been designed or built especially for ourself. But not every one of us is in the financial situation to buy such things. A way out of this dilemma is mass customization. Vendors of mass products recognized the desire of being unique and give potential customers the possibility to create customer specific variants of standard products. Example Nike© offers individual customization of shoes. Today every one of us creates his own individual smartphone by the subscription of specific content or by the installation of individual apps.

2.3 Consumerization

Consumerization refers the desire to use products that have been invented and used by business customers for private purposes. Examples are fax or computers. As a consequence, today companies e.g. rethink their IT-Strategy and establish

Fig. 1 Social collaboration

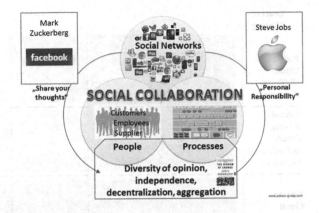

regulations and processes to support principles like "bring your own device" instead of centralized IT-support.

2.4 Everything as a Service (XaaS)

Why do I have to buy computer hardware, software licenses and to build up the know-how of application management and user support if I e.g. would like to use an enterprise resource planning solution? With this question, most enterprises without a background as IT service providers are on the way to an outsourcing service strategy. The following figure shows a market segmentation of Forrester of IT service offerings (Fig. 2).

These megatrends have an impact on business process management as described in the next paragraph.

3 BPM: From Standard to Individualization

3.1 Business Process Management

Business Process Management (BPM) has enabled many organizations over the last 25 years to become more structured, transparent and standardized. In this context, the meaning of standardization is to define normative procedures to manage and organize a company (e.g. for processing a sales order or a purchase order).

By the creation of "ARIS Architecture for Integrated Information Systems" in 1991, A.-W. Scheer created and formalized a process oriented architecture to describe business information systems. The core of ARIS, the metamodel "ARIS House", describes methods and models for different views on business processes like organization, data, function, control and product. Although the technologies to

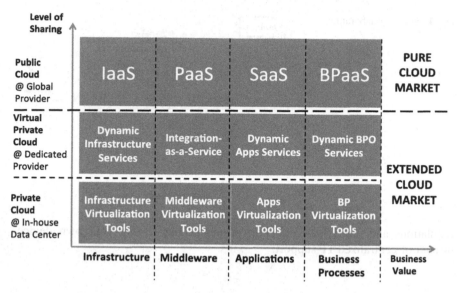

Fig. 2 Market view of Forrester Research© (2010)

implement this architecture were not available at that time, it became a success as an implementation independent modeling approach and for process-oriented introduction of enterprise resource planning systems (Scheer 1990). Even today many concepts of the ARIS Architecture influence the standardization of process modeling.

With the introduction of "ARIS—House of Business Engineering" in 1998 (Scheer 1996) as a life cycle-concept for Business Process Management and the appearance of process integration, transformation, automation and monitoring technologies, the 'process of process management' was standardized and became a crucial part of the configuration of standard business software, system integration, and for the development of individual software.

Even if standardization is still an important topic for organizations, the process of process management has also to comply with the upcoming megatrends. This will be discussed in the next chapter.

3.2 From Process Standard to Individualization

Designing business process models today assumes that all information needed for the model can be gathered at design time. A specific organizational unit is often set up for business process management, which uses modeling methods like BPMN or EPC to gather, arrange and communicate knowledge about the company's business processes. Many organizations have been able to eradicate the chaos of historically evolved business procedures and made them more structured, transparent and standardized.

Following this assumption, the process models serve either as guidelines for customizing standard software (e.g. ERP) or will be transformed in an executable cross-system process description.

But this assumption is wrong for all cases where business processes are weakly structured, multi-variant or simply to be established ad-hoc at run time. Reflecting the megatrends in chapter Collaborative and Social: The real potential behind the cloud, social collaborations will decide at run time who is doing what in a process. Processes will be mass customized at run time to the customer needs and processes can be sourced at any time as a service.

It might theoretically be possible to define a model at design time for any variant or exception, but the implementation will lead to a very complex information system that violates two key criteria for the efficiency of BPM: accelerated processing time and improved user productivity. Some BPM tools and ad-hoc workflow systems have already ran into this issue. However a comprehensive new BPM approach has not yet been developed.

3.3 Production Planning and Control as a Pattern?

As discussed earlier, process models today follow the assumption that individual process instances follow this model. However, this is rarely the case. Looking on discrete manufacturing, the production process for customizable products differs from execution to execution. Processes will be dynamically planned and scheduled by production planning systems. The requirements for the execution of a manufacturing process will be calculated from customer orders and sales forecasts and broken down into preconfigured executable work schedules, which could also be described as a process model. Thus the production planning and control (PPC) approach enables the process adaption and optimization at run time.

But until today, the production planning and control approach is only used for manufacturing process, although the characteristics of business processes and production processes converge. These characteristics can be summarized in the following way:

Business processes become

- **Cyberphysical**: Processes interact with physical objects and cloud-based services that communicate with each other.
- **Predictive**: Planning, forecasting and re-configuration of present and future business by processing process information in real time (big data).
- **Social**: Knowledge-based collaboration of business process owners and users.
- **Mobile**: Operational processes managed in real time from everywhere.

Different research projects like 'ADiWa—Alliance for the digital flow of goods' or the software cluster research project "EMERGENT" examined technologies to implement processes with the characteristics mentioned above. But there is not yet a new holistic and BPM approach to manage processes with these characteristics.

This holistic approach requires a radical change in the focus of BPM: the core aim has to shift away from the definition of typical standard procedures towards supporting the planning of individual processes at run time and to support new paradigms as industry 4.0. The following chapter outlines this type of approach.

3.4 Business Process Planning and Control

As a consequence of this shift production planning and control will now be assigned to all business processes types below and thus generalized. The first two circles in Fig. 3 describe common practices of BPM. However they have (a) less weight and (b) new functions. A standard business process on type level describes one example instance, which is one more or less suitable base solution (template) for the instance descriptions. To respond more precisely to the variability of the instance levels, variants of the typical procedure can be defined, which make it easier to create instances. As with PPC, a planning control center can use standard descriptions to undertake capacity, time and cost planning for the medium-term. However, the process can be respecified (modeled) by creating a business process instance to be executed (with an order release, as it is). This is the heart of the Business Process Planning and Control (BPPC) architecture, suggested by Prof. A.-W. Scheer in (2012). The individual structure of an executable process is now composed, with or without the use of process models as template. It does not contain anything superfluous and also incorporates elements not contained in the standard. Overall, there is greater flexibility in instance description. The individual processes are then managed and controlled by the process control center.

The use of optimization algorithms determines the sequences of process steps and allocation to workstations. Employee-centric criteria can thus be included. Also, depending on the situation, in addition to algorithmic optimization, staff can be given the freedom of self-monitoring. Flexible forms of processing can also be supported by the use of collaborative platforms.

Monitoring functions in the control center make the current process situation transparent and available. The latest model-driven software technologies translate models straight into workable code. Consequently, this dispenses with the need to customize standard software.

The whole process situation to be implemented is available for all authorized personnel. An immediate response can be provided for unscheduled events by redesigning process instances or by new control instructions. Changes can be executed immediately by model-driven software development. Capacity, time and cost situations are up-to-date and transparent. The alternative process models arising over time as a result of redesign can be stored and evaluated. Overall, BPM now focuses mainly on the realization of individually composed process instances.

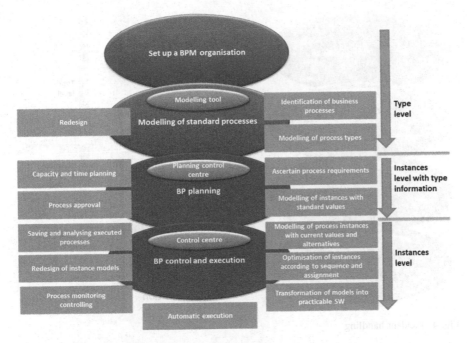

Fig. 3 Business process planning and control (BPPC)

The advantages of Business Planning and Control will be explained on example of a smart home scenario.

4 Example: InDiNet—Smart Home Scenario

In context of the InDiNet research project a generic help desk service has been implemented as a BPaaS solution realizing the core concepts described above. The help desk service can be easily integrated in different service scenarios and adapted to given requirements. For demonstration purposes the help desk service was adapted for the target group of facility managers. The prime responsibility of facility manager services is to quickly respond to faults in heating systems or other household appliances. Thereby, potential problems can be identified differently:

- Automatic reporting of faults due to integrated sensor technology and the discontinuation of a status report.
- Manual reporting of faults using phone, email or web forms (Fig. 4).

Each fault report triggers a new incident management process. On the basis of an established BPM organization this incident management process is first described by a process template at the type level using a suitable modeling tool. At

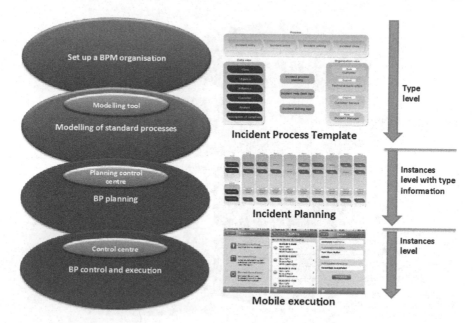

Fig. 4 Incident handling

the instance level each process is being planned individually, using the initial process type information by the planning and control center. Furthermore, each process instance can be adapted during its execution by means of a mobile incident help desk app. The following figure illustrates this approach (Fig. 5).

4.1 Modeling of Standard Processes

For the described showcase the template for the incident management process was created using the Scheer Process Tailor—a SaaS solution, which supports the approach of Business Process Tailoring completely. The incident management process template was derived from the reference process provided by the IT Management Library (ITIL) (2011). This reference process was adapted on the example of manual fault detection. In case of an error, an incident can be recorded manually via a simple web form. In addition to the costumer data, the analyst and the actual description of symptoms, the effect and impact of the fault, as well as the urgency of eliminating the error will be identified. Based on this information, the further routing of this new incident ticket is being determined according to the current defined Service Level Agreements (SLAs). For the technical implementation or rather the representation of these SLAs, modeled and adaptable guidelines are utilized (cf. Fig. 6).

The following roles are involved in the process (Table 1).

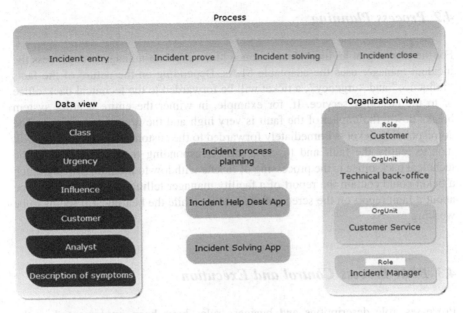

Fig. 5 Incident process template

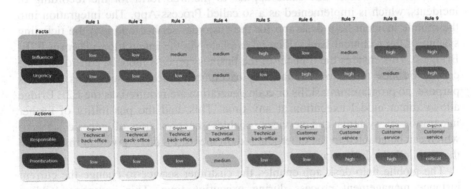

Fig. 6 Incident routing

Table 1 Involved roles

Role	Tasks
Incident manager	• Booking of a generic help desk service (BPaaS) • Customizing incident management process • Definition of the service level agreements
Customer service	• Executive role at medium to high priority tickets • User of the mobile front end for fault finding and removal
Technical back-office	• Second level support at low to medium priority

4.2 Process Planning

For the planning of an individual instance of the incident management process the incident manager uses the adaptable SLAs. Depending on the nature of the facts "influence" and "urgency", a ticket will be forwarded to the technical back-office or to the customer service. If, for example, in winter the entire heating system breaks down, the impact of the fault is very high and the urgency is a given. The corresponding ticket is immediately forwarded to the customer service, whose task it is to rectify the fault and to close the corresponding ticket. The task of the technical back-office is the processing of tickets with low to medium priority. Such a ticket could contain the report of a facility manager telling the customer service about a fault report on the screen of the heating while the heating still seems to be working.

4.3 BPM Process Control and Execution

Processes, role descriptions and business rules have been implemented in the Scheer Process Tailor. The same applies to the web form for the recording of incidents, which is implemented as a so called Process-App. The integration into the mobile incident help desk app for the customer service and into the ticketing system of the technical back-office takes place via the integration platform E2E-Bridge©. This ensures the transfer of the business process models, considering the current business rules to automatically executable process descriptions. For this purpose, no programming skills or code generation are required, as the E2E Bridge allows direct model execution at any time. This, and the possibility of further integration of systems and services, enables the provision of generic services which can be adapted to the emergent requirements. Figure 7 gives an insight into the mobile help desk app.

The mobile help desk app enables the customer service to change the current instance management process during execution time. This comprises adding required process steps which are not included in the initial process template. Each incident management process can be adapted to the current situation and specific requirements individually. This allows a high level of flexibility.

In regards to controlling, the actual data of the running processes are recorded and compared with the agreed SLAs. The data collected is used as a proof that the SLAs were met. Furthermore, the information about the executed processes flows into the knowledge base and is used for continuous improvement of processes in a new design cycle and therefore the modeling of standard processes.

Fig. 7 Mobile help desk app

5 Outlook

The performance of a company is increasingly measured by its ability to develop products and services individually customized to the requirements of its clients and with regard to the processes involved as a service. For this purpose, it is necessary to answer once more and individually the traditional questions of Business Process Management "Who makes what, when, in what quality and using which software applications?" for each process instance. Traditional BPM approaches and solutions reach their limits right from the start as these only capture normative processes. For example, one topic in the discussion of the 4th industrial revolution, that discrete manufacturers have to manage an average size of order from one piece. So every production order has to follow its own process variant. To manage this wealth of variants, approaches like "process tailoring" have been developed. This approach is supported by the 'Scheer Process Tailor' ©, a software solution of Scheer Management GmbH.

Another gap these process variants fail to bridge is efficiently moving from business process design to business process execution.

Business applications are very expensive in terms of time and IT resources if they have to be developed in a traditional way. To avoid this, every business uses eMails, spreadsheets or even paper in different ways and consequently there is no overview of these barely structured processes. This can lead to significant disadvantages in terms of performance and competition, both from a business and IT perspective.

ProcessApps are closing the gap from process design to process execution. Each process can be executed immediately in a simple way. With a few clicks business people are able to create ProcessApps to support people centric processes without support of the IT organization.

An example of an emergent business process implementation is the software service "help desk service" of the InDiNet service platform. It describes a smart way of planning and controlling adaptive business processes.

In the future, the relevance of BPM Tools that support business process planning and control will rise. They will close the gap between business process design and business process execution like production planning and control applications in the area of discrete manufacturing. The approach allows to provide for all contingencies and ad hoc events.

References

Forrester Research Inc. (2010) The evolution of cloud computing markets

ITIL V3 Edition 2011 (2011) Service operations, TSO London

Scheer A-W (1990) Wirtschaftsinformatik. Referenzprozesse für industrielle Geschäftsprozesse. Springer

Scheer A-W (1996) ARIS-House of Business Engineering: Von der Geschäftsprozeßmodellierung zur Workflow-gesteuerten Anwendung; vom Business Process Reengineering zum Continuous Process Improvement. Institut für Wirtschaftsinformatik an der Universität des Saarlandes. Heft 133

Scheer A-W, Feld T, Caspers R (2012) BPM: new architecture driven by Business Process Planning and Control (BPPC). IM J Inf Manage Consult

Towards Security Solutions for Emergent Business Software

Rachid El Bansarkhani, Sascha Hauke and Johannes Buchmann

Abstract Emergent Business Software is highly dynamic and flexible. Monolithic security solutions cannot secure the service composites that this new paradigm enables. Instead, different security services have to be combined in order to provide flexible security solutions. In this paper, we present two concepts that contribute to securing Emergent Business Applications: reputation-based trust mechanisms and secure data aggregation.

1 Introduction

Emergent Business Applications are highly dynamic and flexible composites of a multitude of individual services. Each individual service may even be provided by a different vendor. Furthermore, in order to meet the complex demands of digital enterprises, it adjusts itself autonomously to changes of the market environment and the underlying business models and processes. Emergent software supports diverse and distributed networks of enterprises and is a key enabler for innovative service provisioning in the future internet.

The individual services that constitute an emergent software composite can represent a wide variety of different service types, which include digital services, such as cloud storage, compute services, and information systems for enterprise

R. E. Bansarkhani (✉) · S. Hauke · J. Buchmann
Technische Universität Darmstadt, Fachbereich Informatik, Hochschulstraße 10 64289
Darmstadt, Germany
e-mail: elbansarkhani@cdc.informatik.tu-darmstadt.de

S. Hauke
e-mail: shauke@tk.informatik.tu-darmstadt.de

J. Buchmann
e-mail: buchmann@cdc.informatik.tu-darmstadt.de

G. Brunetti et al. (eds.), *Future Business Software*,
Progress in IS, DOI: 10.1007/978-3-319-04144-5_6,

resource planning, to name just a few. Beyond these, complex business processes also demand the inclusion of real-world, physical services. Physical services are, for instance, production services for custom manufacturing or logistics services for shipping of goods and resources. Furthermore, individual emergent software components are running on systems that can range from wireless sensor nodes, for example for monitoring product shipments, to full-blown data centers that host complex, integrated enterprise services.

As a consequence, emergent business applications vary considerably in their structure, depending not only on their application area, but also on their specific instantiation during runtime. In fact, the same functionality may be supplied by different emergent service compositions. Their flexibility means that they may even change from execution to execution. Securing emergent service compositions, with various services interacting to provide a value-added overall service, poses a considerable challenge.

An intuitive step to solve this task might be to analyze each possible instantiation and try to provide an appropriate pre-selected security solution. This, however, is not realistic. A one-size-fits-all security solution that guarantees end-to-end security is near impossible to achieve in monolithic systems that undergo exhaustive testing. A system whose composition is known definitively only at runtime requires a highly flexible and dynamic security solution itself.

Therefore, it is unavoidable to follow a divide-and-conquer principle, which aims at a structural decomposition of the emergent software approach. From this decomposition, specific security needs have to be derived and met by specialized security solutions. When assembling a new emergent service composition, a new custom security solution can in turn be assembled and deployed. This requires that the individual components are designed securely and that the selection of and interaction between the components is conducted in a secure manner.

To illustrate this exemplarily, consider a simple scenario: A company (vendor) with no production capabilities wishes to produce a product on-demand from its sales portfolio using an ERP system. This ERP service is connected with a billing unit and a manufacturer who is ordered to supply the product. Furthermore, the vendor can choose a transport service, typically a Logistics Service Provider, which is commissioned to transport the goods from the manufacturer to the vendor immediately after completing the production orders. Secure Emergent software applications could provide further options to ensure a reliable and successful processing and transport. This might be attained by an embedded reputation system that helps at assessing the different manufacturers and Logistics Service Providers. Based on the reputation values one can make the best possible choice that guarantees a highly flexible and reliable transaction. Moreover, the vendor could select additional features such as the monitoring of the products during the transport via trucks. This can be realized, for example, by a wireless sensor network (WSN) sensing the needed data and transmitting them securely to a base station. The base station can process the data and inform the vendor about the current status. Sensor data should only be accessible to the vendor and the manufacturer. Such services play an important role when transporting perishable products.

1.1 Contribution

In this paper, we will present initial work that addresses two of the numerous challenges of Emergent Business Software. First, we address trust-based service selection, in particular the integration of external indicators of trustworthiness and of supervised methods for trustworthiness assessment. In order to achieve this, a mapping from supervised estimator output to a trust-oriented belief logic representation is presented.

Furthermore, we introduce secure data aggregation protocols for wireless sensor networks within the scope of Emergent scenarios. Secure data aggregation protocols aim at reducing the amount of data transmissions within the network while ensuring security goals, such as confidentiality and integrity.

1.2 Organization

This paper is structured as follows. In Sect. 2 we discuss the trust-based selection of services. In Sect. 3 we present the concept of secure data aggregation protocols for wireless sensor networks. Finally, we provide some concluding remarks in Sect. 4.

2 Trust-Based Service Selection

Future emergent business software has to account for compositions of different services, both virtual and physical. The dynamic (re-)combination of services, each potentially supplied by a different service provider, enables the creation of value-added composite services. This combination, however, requires the selection of the *right* constituent services, both with regard to functional selection criteria and non-functional aspects, such as selecting reliable providers, that perform according to some quality metric.

Some security-related non-functional aspects of constituent services can be ensured using orthodox IT security methods. Secure communications, for instance, can be guaranteed by using strong encryption, and various system properties can be guaranteed by trusted computing methods, such as remote attestation. However, in end-to-end service provisioning scenarios, in which agents, be they software components or actual persons, are involved, the positive outcome of an interaction is influenced by motives of the agents, uncertainty about the (system) environment, and other external and internal effects. Security assessments, that is, an estimate whether or not an interaction will be successful, becomes a probability estimation problem. In other words, if we consider service provisioning to be an interaction between two parties, one providing a service, the other consuming it, we wish to determine how probable it is that the consuming entity will be satisfied with the service provisioning. The increasingly maturing field of *computational trust* [for a review, see (Jøsang et al. 2007; Wang and Vassileva 2007)] addresses these probabilistic aspects of security and trustworthiness through estimation procedures.

The use of such procedures for service selection, particularly for *web* service selection (Wang and Vassileva 2007; Yan and Prehofer 2011), has been one of the driving motivations behind the development of trust and reputation models and systems. The challenges present in web service selection scenarios are, of course, also relevant within the context of selecting constituent services in future emergent business software. After all, the selection of reliable components is of central importance when assembling emergent service composites and guaranteeing their functioning.

Computational trust models provide a grounding for trust assessment within the extended framework of probability theory. A commonly accepted [though somewhat reductionist, cf. (Castelfranchi and Falcone 2000)] point of view holds *trust* to be a "subjective probability with which an agent [the truster] assesses that another agent [the trustee] […] will perform a particular action" (Gambetta 1988). In this paper, we will follow this definition of trust, as well as the notion that trust is a dyadic, directed and conditionally transitive relation. Furthermore, *trust assessment* will refer to the estimation of the trustworthiness of the trustee by the truster, using an appropriate statistical estimator.

In the broadest sense, we consider the decision whether or not to trust as a binary classification problem—a truster classifies a trustee as either trustworthy or untrustworthy. In this sense, trustworthiness classification is a discriminatory problem suitably assigned to statistical learning methods. However, in order to satisfy the definition of trust as a subjective probability (Gambetta 1988), assigning a class label is insufficient. Rather, the goal in trust assessment is estimating the *probability of class membership*, establishing just *how* likely a particular trustee is to be trustworthy.

Thus, the aim of trust assessment is to reliably estimate the probability of the trustee acting in a trustworthy manner in the next interaction with the truster, based upon representative input data. Thus, if $y \in \{0; 1\}$ is the outcome of such a future interaction, the goal is to compute a *conditional* probability $P(y = 1|\mathbf{x})$ given the features $\mathbf{X}$. For binary outputs, it follows that $P(y = 1|\mathbf{x}) = E(y|\mathbf{x})$.

Experience-based Bayesian prediction methods are the mainstay of computational trust models. However, reinforcement learning, prevalent in their model design, still offers room for improvement. The reliance on a single type of predictor (either direct or reputation-mediated experience), for instance, leads to poor generalizability. While better generalizability can be reached by direct modification of the trust model and the introduction of new assumptions and model parameters [compare, e.g., (Hauke et al. 2012)], the resulting increase in model complexity is undesirable. In spite of the drawbacks of experience-based prediction, they still form a pertinent foundation for the evolution of trust assessment methodologies, because of bootstrapping issues and the fact that often only evaluative instead of instructive feedback (Sutton and Barto 1998) is available to support the assessment.

Let us assume that repeated interactions between a truster and a trustee yield a sample $X \in \{0;1\}^n$ of experiences, maintained by the truster, so that $X = \{x_1, x_2, \ldots, x_n\}$. If an experience $x_i = 1$, it is said to be positive, if $x_i = 0$ negative. Under the assumption that the sample $X \sim Bin(n,p)$, the basic prediction model of the trust estimators used in (Jøsang and Ismail 2002; Ries 2009) is a point estimate of the expectation value of a posterior Beta distribution for parameter p. That is, if r and s are the sum of positive and negative experiences between truster and trustee, the probability estimate[1] is $\frac{r+1}{r+s+2}$. Here, the use of the expectation value of the posterior as an appropriate estimator is due to the equality $P(y = 1|\mathbf{x}) = E(y|\mathbf{x})$. The consistency of this estimator follows from the consistency of the mean as an estimator.

This point estimate is subject to *uncertainty*, that is, the reliability of the estimate is contingent on the dispersion of the data in the recorded sample. A key feature used for the formulation of statistics for computing uncertainty is the consistency of the estimator $\frac{r+1}{r+s+2}$. This leads to simple estimators that regard uncertainty as a function of the sample size $n \in \mathbb{N}$, e.g., $\frac{1}{n+1}$ in (Jøsang and Ismail 2002). Accordingly, *certainty*, which simply is 1—*uncertainty*, can be defined as $\frac{n}{n+1}$. The preceding example for a certainty estimator is only an illustrative example, more expressive certainty estimators exist, e.g., (Wang and Singh 2010).

The meaningful combination of different trustworthiness estimates and the logical inference over them require a framework for reasoning. *Subjective Logic* (Jøsang et al. 2007) is a popular choice for reasoning under uncertainty that is inherent in the estimation process. A more recent but similar framework is *CertainLogic* (Ries 2011), which is derived from and fully isomorphic to *Subjective Logic*.

Within the scope of the Software Cluster projects EMERGENT and INDINET, we model the integration of trust estimates using *CertainLogic*. This choice is governed primarily by the fact that the opinion representation of *CertainLogic* corresponds more intuitively to the outputs and error estimates of the regression machines. Choosing *CertainLogic* over *Subjective Logic* should not be understood as a reflection on the capabilities of each; rather, we believe that using the *CertainLogic* opinion representation will ease understanding.

CertainLogic is derived from *Subjective Logic* and is therefore rooted in belief theory (Shafer 1976). As such, it allows not only for the modelling, combination and inference over probabilities, but over so-called *opinions*. Opinions allow expressing any possible *uncertainty* regarding the probabilities. Ries et al. (2011) propose to represent opinions as ordered triples $\omega = (t, c, f)$, where:

---

[1] We present a basic version here; (Jøsang and Ismail 2002; Ries 2009) allow for a further parameterisation of the prediction model.

- $t \in [0; 1]$ is a *probability estimate* that $y = 1$.
- $c \in [0; 1]$ is a *certainty estimate* that the probability estimate t is correct.
- $f \in [0; 1]$ is a *base rate*, modelling an a priori assumption.

This opinion representation serves as a record for communicating trust estimates, as well as combining them or drawing inferences. Within the projects EMERGENT and INDINET, a number of advances were developed, that are specifically designed to address the creation of trust assessment ensembles and alleviating the market-entry problem faced by new providers. Work has been conducted on extending *CertainLogic* with more flexible operators to combine different opinions (Habib et al. 2012) and on providing tool support for facilitating the integration of trust and reputation systems—specifically, by providing an open source SDK for *CertainTrust* and a deployment tool for assembling such systems (Magin 2013).

2.1 Indicators of Trustworthiness

Suppose that a vendor assembling a composite service, as in Fig. 1, needs to select a specific component service, e.g., one particular logistics company for delivering goods, from a number of competing services. Suppose further that the resulting selection pool contains those services that are claiming to meet the vendor's demands with regard to service level and price. In this context, the question arises: Which specific service provider should be chosen?

If the vendor has enough information about the individual logistics service providers, in particular with regard to their past performance, one might intuitively assert that it should choose the one provider with which the vendor has had the best experience. Thus, the vendor would *preferentially select* the provider with the best reputation or trust score, as computed by an appropriate statistic furnished by an experience-based trust model. However, this requires that sufficient data is available for a reliable trust estimate, ideally for each of the logistics providers, in order for the vendor to make an informed decision.

If no prior experience are available to the vendor, either through direct dealings in the past or via recommendations, the decision by the vendor is reduced to a purely explorative selection process, with no prior knowledge to exploit. This *bootstrap* problem of experience-based trust models brings about increased risk inherent in the selection process for the vendor (as the truster). At the same time, lack of information also represents a handicap for the service providers (as trustees). They had no opportunity to represent their competencies and trustworthiness. Especially when some providers have already managed to build a good reputation, new providers will be at a considerable disadvantage. They face a *market entry* problem. This can have negative consequences for both truster and trustee: The truster may not chose the optimal trustee, while the trustee might never be selected.

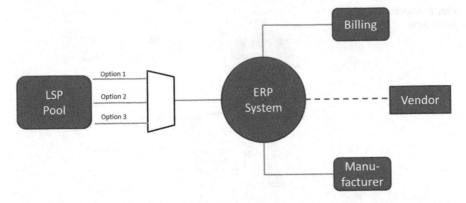

Fig. 1 Real scenario for emergent software application

In this scenario, *indicators of trustworthiness* can be helpful to both truster and trustee by alleviating the issues outlined above. An indicator of trustworthiness is a feature of the trustee that signifies that it will behave as expected by the truster. Examples of such indicators can, for instance, be a *certificate* issued by a trusted certification agency, an *insurance* against service delivery failure or *coalition* with other known trustees in other contexts, for which trust information is available to the truster. We have explicitly modelled these indicators as extensions of the *CertainTrust* model in (Hauke et al. 2012). However, extending the specific model used for statistical inference tends to bloat it and make it unwieldy by necessitating a dedicated extension per (class of) indicator/feature. Additionally, it does not improve the generalizability of the Bayesian experience-based trust model to the degree desired and required in emergent service environments, as it merely assumes delegation of trust between a known entity (such as an insurer or certifier) and an unknown entity (the trustee under evaluation).

As a consequence, trust estimation ensembles were investigated that combine experience-based Bayesian trust estimators, rooted in reinforcement learning, with supervised trust estimators that provide feature-based generalizability. In order to assemble these ensembles in a flexible manner, *CertainLogic* (Ries et al. 2011) was extended with new fusion operations (Habib et al. 2012).

2.2 Supervised Trust Assessment

A key argument behind the introduction of experience-based computational trust modelling was the scarcity of traditional cues related to trustworthiness in computer mediated interactions (Jøsang et al. 2007). An indicator of trustworthiness can be thought of as a feature or set of features that a trustee possesses that are supposedly representative of its trustworthiness. While *traditional cues*, that serve as indicators and are learned from interactions in brick-and-mortar environments,

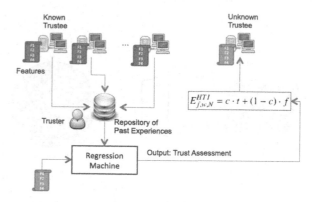

Fig. 2 Supervised trust assessment

often cannot be applied to online interactions, modern online services expose a wealth of observable features. These can form the basis for learning new cues, which in turn can provide better generalizability for computational trust assessment (Fig. 2).

Data mining approaches for exploiting high-dimensional feature spaces for probability estimation tasks are numerous. Parametric models, such as logistic regression, are traditionally applied there. However, they suffer from considerable drawbacks that limit their use in trust assessment in computer mediated interactions. In particular, parametric models have to be specifically fitted to the problem they are to address. In order to avoid model misspecification, predictors and supposed interrelations have to be input correctly. This limits their use considerably considering the scalability and flexibility required in data-rich environments where features can exhibit different scale types, dimensionality, and correlation structures (Malley et al. 2012).

Model-free, non-parametric regression machines support the robust estimation of conditional probabilities from feature sets of different scale types and potentially high dimensionality. They make no distributional assumptions for the vector of features, make no restrictions on the length of the feature list, and do not rely on a specified model as a starting point (Malley et al. 2012). In order to allow for *robust* probability estimation and thereby enable rigorous and meaningful inferences with regard to the trustworthiness of a trustee, consistency of the regression model has to be established. When using a Bayes estimate of the trustworthiness score as regressand, consistency is inherent in the consistent Bayes estimator.

Following (Malley et al. 2012), we treat the probability estimation problem constituted by trust assessment as a *non-parametric regression* problem. Thus, a regression machine will serve to estimate the non-parametric regression function $f(\mathbf{x}) = E(y|\mathbf{x}) = P(y = 1|\mathbf{x})$, where X is a vector of features (regressors). The output of a regression machine, after training on a suitably large training data set, is a probability estimate $P(y = 1|\mathbf{x})$. Additionally, a goodness-of-fit measure can be computed that gives the reliability of the estimate.

Methods of web data extraction, for instance, can be employed for gathering relevant information. However, the *true* regressand—that is, the intrinsic trust-worthiness of the trustee—is an unobservable variable in real-world applications. In its place, a point estimate from an experience-based naive Bayes estimation method can be used. Ideally, this is a robust reputation-based trust model, such as (Jøsang and Ismail 2002; Ries 2009). Due to the mostly academical nature of these works and the consequent absence of their real-world application, widely-used basic reputation systems may have to be substituted instead.

We have tested several types of regression machines on real-world data (Hauke et al. 2013); specifically, random forests, k-nearest neighbour methods, and various decision tree algorithms.

Random forests (Breiman 2001) are non-parametric ensemble classifiers consisting of a multitude of decision trees. They are generally considered to be fast and and accurate classifiers that offer considerably better performance than single trees (Biau and Devroye 2010), for instance, CART(Breiman et al. 1984) or M5 (Quinlan 1992).

In recent publications dealing with the application of machine learning to trustworthiness assessment tasks (Burnett et al. 2010; Liu et al. 2011), decision trees have been used for classification tasks. There are several decision tree algorithms that can perform regression and are suitable for trustworthiness assessment. Specifically, we will test CART (Breiman et al. 1984) and M5 (Quinlan 1992) decision tree algorithms on the dataset. Decision trees offer white box behaviour and interpretability of the generated models. They are also reasonably robust, performant, and can deal with different scale types as input data.

The goodness-of-fit of the supervised estimators evaluated in (Hauke et al. 2013) did *not* warrant building a standalone trust management system around them. The features of the real world data investigated did not provide sufficient discriminatory power to build accurate models from the skewed data and do not yield reliable trust scores. However, the regression machines still provide if not an accurate fit of the trustworthiness, then at least an *indication* of how trustworthy a particular service (provider) is. As such, they can still be of value within a trustworthiness estimation *ensemble*. They can be used in a supplementary role, for instance as input to the base rate or initial expectation of an experience-based Bayesian model. The flexible mapping of regression machine output to *Certain-Trust* provides a method for harnessing the obtained results within a trust assessment ensemble.

When using regression machines, mapping the probability estimate t is trivially achieved by using the prediction value, as in Bayesian models. Certainty estimation, however, has to be done in a different manner, due to different characteristics and purposes of the prediction paradigm.

We propose using a conservative goodness-of-fit measure, for instance the *normalised root-mean-square error* (*nrmsw*):

Definition 1 Let $O = (o_1, o_2, \ldots, o_n)$ be a vector of observed values and $\hat{S} = (\hat{s}_1, \hat{s}_2, \ldots, \hat{s}_n)$ a vector of corresponding estimates. Let o_{max} be the largest, o_{min} the smallest element of O.

$$nrmse = \frac{\left(\sqrt{\frac{1}{n}\sum_{i=1}^{n}(\hat{s}_i - o_i)^2}\right)}{(o_{max} - o_{min})}$$

The mapping from estimator output to the *CertainLogic* opinion space is thus given as:

- $t = P(y = 1|\mathbf{x})$
- $c = 1 - (min(nrmse, 1))$
- $f \in [0; 1]$, a (user defined) default base rate to be used under complete uncertainty, e.g., 0.5.

While supervised methods do not entirely solve the bootstrap and market-entry problem inherent in reputation-based trust, they provide additional generalisation and ease the burden of establishing a history of individual experiences for each trustee. Identifying and promoting the adoption of indicators with high discriminatory power remains a challenge. Current certification schemes, such as certificates issued by standardisation bodies, still contain too little explanatory information in order to be used as standalone, supervised trust assessment models. However, with the increasing understanding behind the technical, as well as the socio-economic mechanisms of trust and reputation, that results from the application and proliferation of trust systems, we are confident that expressive indicators of trustworthiness can be derived. Particularly in the context of future emergent business software, in which large amounts of data are going to be generated that can be leveraged for trust assessment, for instance by furnishing features that can serve as indicators of trustworthiness, supervised methods can play an important role in imbuing generalizability in trust models.

3 Secure Data Aggregation

In the following section we focus on a service that allows a vendor and the manufacturer to monitor the products during the transport by means of a WSN.

A characteristic feature of sensor nodes is the well-known fact that data transmissions consume a lot of energy. According to (Hill et al. 2000), sending a single bit consumes as much battery power as executing 800 to 1,000 instructions. Indeed, this has an adverse impact on the nodes that are located near to the base station. A reason for this is the huge amount of messages to be forwarded from the rest of the network. This, of course, leads to a higher battery power consumption.

As such, there is an inherent need for decreasing the amount of traffic in order to prolong the lifetime of the WSN. Therefore, it would be beneficial to swap communication costs for computation costs. In many applications, the base station collects all data and applies simple functions on the transmitted data. For instance, functions, such as the computation of sums and the average of temperatures, are more interesting in applications than considering each value on its own. This raises the question whether it is possible to delegate such simple computations to some dedicated nodes having the capabilities to carry out this task. Such a mechanism is achieved in data aggregation protocols which aim at reducing the amount of transmitted messages.

An aggregation protocol involves mainly three parties: The user initiates a request for a fresh data of choice. The base station is responsible for distributing the query within the network. An aggregator node has mainly the tasks to collect the sensed data from a subset of nodes, applying the aggregation function on this data, and finally forwarding the aggregation value towards the base station. Of course, it is also possible that aggregator nodes lying between the base station and other aggregator nodes apply the same function on the aggregation results of their predecessors. In the literature one can find a great deal of such aggregation protocols which can be classified in the manner the packets are routed through the WSN. Basically, there exist tree-based and cluster-based approaches. Of course, hybrid variants are also conceivable. See (Ozdemir and Xiao 2009) for an overview.

Regarding the basic scenario, where the vendor wishes to monitor the transport of its products via trucks, it is more convenient to consider a cluster-based topology. Each truck forms a cluster consisting of a number of sensor nodes and a dedicated cluster-head. The sensor nodes, so called leafs, send their data to the cluster-head which takes over the task of the aggregator node and thus transmits the aggregation result to the base station (See Fig. 3). The leafs could sense the temperature of perishables or the humidity in the truck, to name a few examples. Furthermore, the communication within the WSN should be protected from eavesdropping. The vendor and the manufacturer are the only institutions authorized to have access to the data. This obviously implies to apply secure data aggregation protocols, which aim at securing the communication channels within the WSN. In general, it has to be assessed which security goals are most required for the scenarios in consideration. For instance, in many use cases confidentiality plays a minor role, whereas the protection of the freshness and integrity of the data as well as an authenticated source of the data are mandatory goals in the context of WSN. This is due to an easier physical access to the sensor nodes and the openness of WSNs enabling any person to manipulate the traffic. When transmitting sensed data without applying any security solutions, it is very easy to inject forgeries into the WSN. One way to do this is to compromise a sensor node or an aggregator node. Therefore, it is common to consider security models taking into account node capture attacks.

Secure data aggregation protocols are primarily classified into the plaintext-based aggregation and the ciphertext-based aggregation approaches. Plaintext-based methods focus on securing the communication channel in a hop-by-hop

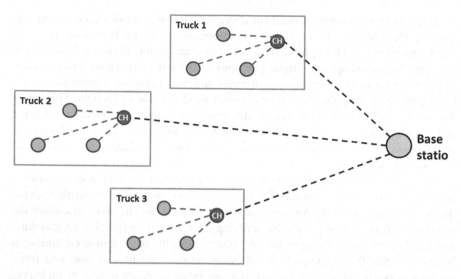

Fig. 3 Real scenarion using secure data aggregation techniques

manner. This means that any aggregator node receiving encrypted packets from sensor nodes computes the aggregation value on the decrypted plaintext-data before forwarding ciphertext on the aggregation value. In our case the cluster head collects the encrypted data from its cluster members and decrypts them in order to compute the aggregation result. Afterwards, the clusterhead encrypts the value and forwards it towards the base station. As opposed to this, ciphertext-based approaches provide end-to-end security. Aggregation tasks are performed on the ciphertext rather than on the plaintext.

For the above scenario one can use AES together with the EAX mode (Bellare et al. 2003) providing simultaneously confidentiality and data authentication. AES is a symmetric key encryption scheme which is very efficient and thus suitable for practical applications. The EAX mode provides a mechanism for data source authentication.

4 Conclusion

Here, we presented our work in progress on reputation-based trust and secure data aggregation as security components in future emergent business environments. In conjunction with other emergent security components, they are en- visioned to contribute to the flexible security required in Emergent Business Software. Other technologies that are actively pursued, such as data flow and information flow control, lightweight cryptography, or system integrity and attestation, can be combined with the presented work, for instance, via the policy toolkit (Dinkelaker et al. 2011) developed in EMERGENT. The ultimate goal is to achieve the robustness requirements that the emergent software paradigm necessitates. This work will continue, both academically and in the scope of various projects, such as the BMBF-funded project SINNODIUM.

References

Bellare M, Rogaway P, Wagner D (2003) Eax: a conventional authenticated-encryption mode. IACR Cryptol ePrint Arch 2003:69

Biau G, Devroye L (2010) On the layered nearest neighbour estimate, the bagged nearest neighbor estimate and the random forest method in regression and classification. J Multivar Anal 101:2499–2518

Breiman L (2001) Random forests. Mach Learn 45:5–32

Breiman L, Friedman JH, Olshen RA, Stone CJ (1984) Classification and regression trees. Technical report, Wadsworth and Brooks/Cole Advanced Books and Software

Burnett C, Norman TJ, Sycara K (2010) Bootstrapping trust evaluations through stereotypes. In: Proceedings of 9th international conference on autonomous agents and multiagent systems, pp 241–248

Castelfranchi C, Falcone R (2000) Trust is much more than subjective probability: mental components and sources of trust. In: Proceedings of the 33rd annual Hawaii international conference on system sciences

Dinkelaker T, Eichberg M, Mezini M (2011) Incremental concrete syntax for embedded languages. In: Proceedings of the 2011 ACM symposium on applied computing, SAC '11, New York, NY, USA, pp 1309–1316

Gambetta Diego (1988) Can We Trust Trust? In: Gambetta D (ed) Trust: making and breaking cooperative relations. Basil Blackwell, Oxford, pp 213–237

Habib SM, Ries S, Hauke S, Mühlhäuser M (2012) Fusion of opinions under uncertainty and conflict—trust assessment for cloud marketplaces. In: Proceedings of IEEE TrustCom-12

Hauke S, Volk F, Habib SM, Mühlhäuser M (2012) Integrating indicators of trustworthiness into reputation-based trust models. In: Proceedings of the 6th IFIP WG 11.11 international conference, IFIPTM 2012

Hauke S, Biedermann S, Mühlhäuser M, Heider D (2013) On the application of supervised machine learning to trustworthiness assessment. Technical Report TUD-CS-2013-0050, TR-014, Technische Universität Darmstadt

Hill J, Szewczyk R, Woo A, Hollar S, Culler D, Pister K (2000) System architecture directions for networked sensors. In: Proceedings of the 9th international conference on Architectural support for programming languages and operating systems, ASPLOS IX, New York, NY, USA, pp 93–104. ACM

Jøsang A, Ismail R (2002) The beta reputation system. In: Proceedings of the 15th bled electronic commerce conference

Jøsang A, Ismail R, Boyd C (2007) A survey of trust and reputation systems for online service provision. Decis Support Syst 43(2):618–644

Liu X, Trédan G, Datta A (2011) A generic trust framework for large-scale open systems using machine learning. CoRR, abs/1103.0086

Magin S (2013) Engineering a trust management system: a flexible, component-based approach. Master's thesis, TU Darmstadt

Malley JD, Kruppa J, Dasgupta A, Malley KG, Ziegler A (2012) Probability machines: consistent probability estimation using nonparametric learning machines. Methods Inf Med 51(1):74–81

Ozdemir S, Xiao Y (2009) Secure data aggregation in wireless sensor networks: a comprehensive overview. Comput Netw 53:2022–2037

Quinlan JR (1992) Learning with continuous classes. In: Proceedings AI, pp 343–348

Ries S (2009) Extending bayesian trust models regarding context-dependence and user friendly representation. In: Proceedings of the 2009 ACM Symposium on applied computing, New York, USA, pp 1294–1301

Ries S, Habib SM, Mühlhäuser M, Varadharajan V (2011) CertainLogic: a logic for modeling trust and uncertainty (Short Paper). In: Proceedings of the 4th international conference on trust and trustworthy computing (TRUST 2011). Springer

Shafer G (1976) A mathematical theory of evidence. Princeton University Press, Princeton

Sutton RS, Barto AG (1998) Reinforcement learning: an introduction. MIT Press, Cambridge, MA

Wang Y, Singh MP (2010) Evidence-based trust: a mathematical model geared for multiagent systems. ACM Trans Auton Adapt Syst (TAAS) 5(4):14

Wang Y, Vassileva J (2007) Toward trust and reputation based web service selection: a survey. Int Trans Syst Sci Appl 3(2):118–132

Yan Z, Prehofer C (2011) Autonomic trust management for a component-based software system. IEEE Trans Dependable Secure Comput 8(6):810–823

Part III
Agile Software Development

Agile Methods, Lean Development and the Change of Work in Software Development

Andreas Boes and Tobias Kämpf

Abstract For a long time, agile methods such as Scrum and XP have been considered as an innovative niche for specialists in IT. This is changing profoundly. The combination of agile methods and the principles of "Lean Development" has become the foundation for a deep change in the organization of software development in general. Empowered teams, synchronized development processes, collective forms of knowledge and continuous improvement of processes are the central elements of a new state of the art in software development. This evolving organisation of work in the IT sector leads to a new situation for IT employees and to new working conditions. Based on empirical research this paper shows how the work of software developers has changed, which experiences they have made and which challenges they are confronted with.

1 Introduction and State of the Art

Just some years ago, new forms of agile software development, like Scrum, Pair Programming or Test-Driven Development, were considered an innovative experimentation field exclusively for specialists. These methods fascinated many developers from the beginning precisely because they had been explicitly created in opposition to "classical" waterfall models. All the same, for the first years after their creation in the middle of the nineties they remained a niche issue, highly appreciated in the community but not yet introduced into the enterprises. This was especially true for the big companies dominating the IT market.

A. Boes (✉) · T. Kämpf (✉)
ISF München, Jakob-Klar-Str. 9 80796 Munich, Germany
e-mail: Andreas.Boes@isf-muenchen.de

T. Kämpf
e-mail: tobi.kaempf@isf-muenchen.de

G. Brunetti et al. (eds.), *Future Business Software*,
Progress in IS, DOI: 10.1007/978-3-319-04144-5_7,
© Springer International Publishing Switzerland 2014

This picture has changed profoundly since then, according to the current state of the art of research on agile methods (cf. for instance Dingsøyr et al. 2010; Sutherland and Schwaber 2011). Agile methods have made their way on a large scale in the IT world. They are now being applied area wide, even in the big companies, e.g. Google, IBM, Microsoft, SAP and Yahoo! (cf. for instance Woodward et al. 2010; Sutherland and Schwaber 2011). This is not only true for English language countries but also for Germany and all of Europe. Or, as the German journal "Computerwoche" already commented in 2010: "The argument between champions of linear and agile software development is now water under the bridge. The paradigm shift is in full swing" (Computerwoche 2010).

Against this backdrop we intend to ask the question how this remarkable triumph of agile methods can be explained. We argue that their breakthrough in the companies has been enabled by combining them with the principles of "Lean Development", and that this combination currently entails a fundamental change in the organization of software development. From a sociology of work view we shall notably focus on the employees' perspective, outlining the changes in their work environment that result from this breakthrough. We draw on several empirical research projects that enabled us to investigate the changes in the IT industry during the last decade from different points of view.[1] In addition, we have scientifically accompanied the introduction of lean and agile methods in a leading European IT firm for the last 3 years, doing intensive research about it.

2 Fundamental Change in Software Development

The increasing proliferation and pervasion of agile methods in leading IT companies indicates a fundamental change in software development. To understand this change it is no longer sufficient to study the original principles laid down in the Agile Manifesto. Rather, the triumph of agile methods proves to be a dynamic process that actually implies a shift of the context of agile methods. It is especially the link to new concepts of "lean development" that leads to a new situation: agile methods, now widely accepted, open up new ways for an industrialization of software development in the context of "lean".

---

[1] Most notably the projects funded by the Federal Ministry of Education and Science, "GlobePro" (www.globe-pro.de, 2009–2013), "Women in Career" (www.frauen-in-karriere.de, 2008–2013), "pinowa" (www.pinowa.de, 2012–2015), "Diwa-IT" (www.diwa-it.de, 2007–2010), and "Export IT" (www.export-it.de, 2005–2009). On the whole, we have done several hundreds of expert interviews and intensive interviews with employees and managers in this context (cf. e.g. Boes et al. 2011a, 2012; Kämpf et al. 2011).

2.1 Stages of Development: From the "Agile Manifesto" to "Lean Development"

Against this backdrop it makes sense to look back, historically reconstructing the rise of agile methods. Three significant stages of development can be differentiated:

Pioneer stage: In the middle of the 1990s, pioneers like Ken Schwaber, Mike Beedle, Kent Beck, Alistair Cockburn or Jeff Sutherland began to come up with new methods for software development, which were finally conceived as "agile methods". Their starting point was a fundamental criticism of bureaucratic concepts of software development as they then prevailed in the enterprises in the form of the "waterfall model" as the dominant type of project management. These concepts implied a strictly sequential process and particularly a clear separation of specification and coding. In practice, rigid project management, tight time schedules, tense budgets and formalization of development work led to increasing restrictions of the developers' scope of action. On the whole, this procedure proved to be hardly successful—neither with respect to the quality of software nor to the plannability of many software projects. Typically, many problems only arose in the last stage of development which caused serious delay or even total failure of big projects (cf. for instance DeMarco and Lister 1987). A frequent company response to these imponderabilities was to install even more formalization, division of work, and rigid project management. Consequently, criticism and discomfort grew among developers and IT specialists. Many of them got the feeling that the organizational models did not fit to what they considered to be the essence of their work, constraining and even obstructing them by the rising tide of formal processes. Moreover, the priorities within the projects became increasingly controversial: Should they still focus upon excellent code and genuine customer benefit, or exclusively upon economically defined "milestones" and KPIs? These experiences ultimately formed the background and resonance chamber for the pioneering stage of agile methods. Here the IT community's criticism of growing bureaucratization and standardization of software development found an expression—in the sense of a social movement, as it were. This special characteristic very clearly asserted itself in the central principles of the Agile Manifesto, finally published in 2001, in sentences like: "*individuals and interactions over processes and tools*" or "*responding to change over following a plan*" (www.agile-manifesto.com).

Grassroot stage: After the publication of the Agile Manifesto a new stage began to evolve. Emanating from pioneer companies that specifically applied agile methods, they began to find ways into the world of enterprises. This diffusion process was driven by an increasing number of small consulting firms specializing in the new methods. Their application was no longer restricted to small and medium sized enterprises, but big enterprises started to test them in pilot projects as well. Such pilot projects were frequently still initiatives of individual project leaders who were enthusiastic about the new models, e.g. organizing single software teams according to Scrum principles. The wider organizational structures of the companies were not yet touched, however. It was especially Scrum that became a catchword or quasi-synonym for agile methods. While the employees usually responded positively, the management remained skeptical in the beginning. But when first results proved to be positive, open-mindedness and interest also grew on the part of the management. The increasing attention paid by the management gave rise to new questions and challenges. For instance, how is it possible to scale agile methods and to organize not only a few teams but development departments with several thousand employees according to Scrum? Are models like Scrum or Pair Programming functional for a globally distributed organization as well?

New production model: In the grassroot stage, agile methods had only been applied punctually in big IT companies, whereas now their company-wide breakthrough ensued. First and foremost in the form of Scrum they were introduced in the big IT and software companies on a large scale and in the course of big reorganization processes. The crucial success factor for this breakthrough was the linkage to ideas of Lean Management resp. the embedding of agile methods into new forms of Lean Development. "Lean" not only gives new answers to the question of scale but in the context of "lean" agile methods also gained a new compatibility to central strategic management objectives and ideas—not least in a semantic sense. This holds true not only for the target of increasing efficiency but also with respect to the transparency, control and planning of development units made up of numerous employees. In this regard, particularly the high dependency upon individual key-players with special knowledge had been identified as a problem. A new solution to this problem was seen especially in Scrum with its strong focus on teamwork and short-cycled intervals of development. For this reason, Scrum prevailed as the new organization model of software teams in "lean" concepts of development. The changes involved are not to be underestimated. Indeed the combination of lean development and agile methods gives rise to a new state of the art of software development. This new model of production fundamentally alters the way how software development is organized in IT companies. On the one hand, the abandoning of old waterfall concepts and the failure of bureaucratic-tayloristic approaches become manifest. On the other hand, through the combination with "lean", IT work simultaneously gets open to alternative concepts of industrialization standing for a new "type of industrialization" (cf. Boes 2004; Boes and Kämpf 2012)

2.2 Software Development in a New Production Model

The ideas of Lean Production have their origin in the Japanese automotive industry (cf. fundamentally Womack et al. 1991). The new concepts of industrialization developed in this context have been revolutionizing production worldwide since the middle of the 1980s. Meanwhile they are being increasingly transferred to work areas like administration, research and development and last not least IT (cf. e.g. Poppendieck and Poppendieck 2003, 2007; Middleton and Sutton 2005; Morgan and Liker 2006; Reinertsen 2009; Westkämper and Sihn 2010). A systemic understanding of production processes makes up the core of "Lean". Whereas traditional concepts rely on rationalization of single work activities, "lean" focuses upon the systemic optimization and organization of the process as a whole. The complete value chain—from development to customer delivery—is considered from a holistic point of view. Each individual link of the chain but also their mutual interplay is continuously questioned and (when applicable) optimized as to its contribution to the value-added and the customer benefit. The various principles and methodologies of "Lean", as kanban, avoidance of waste ("muda") or focus upon continuous improvement ("kaizen"), are based on this conceptual framework.

This basic idea of systemic integration is an essential starting point for the new production model. Software development is now conceptualized as a systemically integrated value chain geared towards the joint production of customer benefit. Consequently, a consistent process orientation gains in importance. Whereas development units were traditionally often characterized by uncontrolled growth, the intention is now that general processes form the backbone of a homogeneous organization. Software development is to be organized as an "objective process" that no longer solely relies on the knowledge and motivation of individual employees. However, the new model does not resort to the rigid standards and process models of the past but seeks to establish "intelligent processes" structuring work and cooperation systemically while at the same time permitting the individuals involved to effectively apply their special competence and creativity to the value-added. Therefore, the processes have to be flexible and open to continuous questioning and optimizing. Process orientation becomes the basis of collective learning in the companies. Thus, the principle of continuous improvement that is a vital part of "lean" becomes a cornerstone of the new production model. Closely connected to this principle is the aim to organize software development more in the way of a "collectivization of knowledge." This means to share knowledge in a new quality and to render the existing know-how applicable and available throughout the whole company—which also makes the company less vulnerable and dependent on individual employees' know-how.

On an operative level, we can identify three central elements characterizing the new production model in practice:

First of all, the "empowered team" that becomes the "nucleus" of the new production model. The basic module of organization is no longer the individual software developer but rather a collective team of software developers (cf. Boes et al. 2013). As an autonomous entity, the "team of ten" organizes itself and disposes of considerable leeway in the daily work. Based upon the Scrum principles, the team members can decide themselves how the applications are to be coded and how much they are able to manage in the course of one sprint. The central underlying principle is the team's "commitment." The new importance of the team simultaneously brings about a paradigm shift from the principle of individual expertise to collective domains of knowledge. The team structures and work processes are now characterized by a new quality of knowledge sharing and transparency within the team. Besides new concepts like Pair Programming particularly the routines of meetings, e.g. Daily Scrums, are geared towards this end.

Secondly, the teams' developmental work is organized as a part of a *synchronized value chain*. This is based upon short-cycled intervals of development, replacing project cycles of several months or even years that were valid in the past. Each team now has to deliver "usable software" in a synchronized rhythm of 2–4 weeks' sprints. This is the foundation for a new quality of systemic integration. So, even very big development units with several thousand developers will "swing" in a single rhythm. Supported by modern development environments, the compatibility and interplay of the code produced by many different teams can be tested again and again in an iterative manner—and, what is more, already in a very early stage of the development process. The fundamental importance of the "usable software" principle is most graphically underlined if it is compared with the characteristic (then often unsolvable) problems in the last stages of big waterfall projects, where over a long time many teams, in mutual isolation, develop modules that finally prove incompatible to each other.

Thirdly, through *fragmentation of complex software on the basis of backlogs* big development projects can be organized in division of labor—without systematically or temporally separating the process of specification and architecture of software from the process of coding. On the background of a description of the required software functionalities, a so-called backlog of items is formed which is cascaded downwards, with the "product owners" taking the responsibility towards the respective "teams of ten" that are in charge. In big projects often a stand-alone pyramidal structure of "product owners" is established, who organize the cooperation according to the principle "Scrum of Scrums." Priorization and precise description of the individual items now occur iteratively from sprint to sprint. This new form of structuring ultimately leads to a new kind of transparency as well. Whereas development work previously often remained a black box for outsiders, now it is relatively easy to discern after a sprint which backlog items were successfully settled and to evaluate the overall project status on this basis. Burn-down charts hold the potential for a precise tracking of the progress of work in single teams but also whole departments at any time, even during a sprint. This new transparency is not only the basis for collective learning processes in the teams but also creates new potentials for efficient reporting and controlling of IT work.

3 Change of Work and the Employees' Perspective

Our empirical research indicates that the employees predominantly experience the "lean" reorganization of software development and particularly the implementation of agile methods like Scrum as a step in the right direction. Notably the empowerment of the teams and the rising importance of teamwork are appreciated and considered an improvement. Many employees also expect that abandoning waterfall models will also mean a reduction of "bureaucracy" and "micro management" of software development in the companies. This is an expression of the hope that the proportion of genuine software development will rise again and that the bureaucratic overhead which has been demanding an ever larger part of the developers' daily work will be reduced. From the employees' perspective, in this context the growing customer orientation is also seen as a new chance. After the years of dominance of purely economical thinking and KPI-driven software development, they hope that the focus will return to high-quality software which really benefits the client. And since the growing globalization of software development in the form of "offshoring" over the last years has been experienced as a threat by many developers (cf. Boes et al. 2012; Boes and Kämpf 2006), the increasing re-location of teams-of-ten at one site should not be underestimated as a positive reference point for many employees.

In spite of this basically favorable disposition, there are indications in practice that the extensive changes confront the developers with new challenges and fundamental transformations of their work situation. IT work now becomes "public" in a totally new quality in the context of "lean" (Bultemeier 2011). This "publicity" increasingly forms the basis for cooperation and collective learning. Consequently, software development does no longer occur in "happy solitude" behind closed doors. Rather, development work becomes increasingly transparent and the developers have to act more and more in public spheres. This applies e.g. for regular meetings as Daily Scrum, Sprint Planning or Review. These meetings not only require presentations of work results but also communication of the individual progress in work. Often, this is seen with a critical eye. In such cases, employees would refer to an obligation to "expose themselves" or to "justify themselves."

This "work in public" poses new demands for the developers. No longer is it enough for them to be capable of applying their professional know-how, rather they must also be able to share and communicate it. This requires a change of many developers' mindset: they have to open up and to engage in the new areas of "publicity." However, without a pronounced culture of trust within the companies this requirement cannot be met. Cultures of trust are the main success factor for using publicity as a basis of collective learning. If there is no trust, the new transparency will rather be experienced as a threat, more specifically, as a constituent of increased control and monitoring over the employees. In our empirical research we found that not only conflicts with the management but also conflicts within teams ("peer-group pressure") may considerably increase if trust is missing.

Another central challenge for the employees in the context of the new production model is the transition from individual specialization towards collective domains of knowledge. Whereas the organization of software development previously was built upon the specialized expert with individualized know-how, now companies strive for an increasing collectivization of knowledge which implies the end of "silo-thinking". Younger developers tend to see this as a chance but experienced developers often experience this change of expert modus as decline and debasement. For years they have been concentrating upon their specific area of expertise, often acquiring profound knowledge there. Against this backdrop, the demand to share this treasure with others and to open it up to non-specialists causes resentment and incomprehension with many developers. The reason is not only that they strongly identify with "their" code, considering the software "their baby", but rather that they feel their special expertise, acquired over years, to be disregarded and not acknowledged. Moreover the fact that the employees are losing "unique selling propositions" and control over "areas of uncertainty" (Crozier and Friedberg 1979) in the working process should not be underestimated. From the employees' perspective, a fundamental question is raised here: Could not the new focus upon collective domains of knowledge promote the exchangeability of individual developers, thus considerably weakening their employee position?

With respect to the changes of working conditions implied by the new production model, the question of stress turns out to be an important issue as well. On one hand, "lean" and especially agile methods offer a lot of approaches for promotion of occupational health (Boes et al. 2011b; Boes and Kuntz-Mayr 2009). "Commitment" and team assessment of the work to be expended can be new instruments to put a sustainable work pace in software projects into practice. At the same time, issues like meaning and purpose of work, empowerment of team cultures and also customer orientation may serve to address important "salutogenic" (Antonovsky 1979) potentials. On the other hand, the experiences of employees show that stress often increases in practice. For instance, synchronization and systemic integration may result in a loss of time floats and organizational buffers so that the work load has to be done under the impression of permanent time pressure. Particularly a lack of team empowerment proves to be an important stress factor in this context. In this case the danger arises that the employees feel they have to simply "execute" the backlog like "on the assembly line", without being able to influence the work load or work content in any way. Thus, collective learning loops lose their basis. But we found empirically that even in successful and really empowered teams the realization of salutogenic potentials cannot be taken for granted: without purposeful "slow movement" and a culture of "slack" (Cyert and March 1963), there is the danger that only one-dimensional productivity growth ensues which may lead to short-term success but is hardly sustainable. In a figurative sense, these teams learn "how to run ever faster" but they also should have to learn that it is not good to "always run at full speed." In order to benefit from the health-promoting potentials, specific measures have to be taken. Otherwise new stress factors might seriously endanger the success of the new production model.

4 Outlook: Agile Methods at the Crossroads

The embedding into a new production model has fundamentally changed the point of departure for agile methods. In spite of their wide acceptance and application, the implementation of central principles and ideas of the grassroot stage (e.g. "individuals and interactions over processes and tools") must not be taken for granted in many companies. In order to fill the agile principles with life in practice, commitment will still be needed. The crucial point is that the linkage of agile methods and lean production has changed the strategic context: to put it bluntly, the first priority is no longer to oppose the "bureaucratic waterfall", but rather to establish the agile principles within a new production model.

So agile methods now stand at a fundamental crossroads. On the one hand, we could conceive a scenario where agile methods and the new production model pave the way for a better use and acknowledgement of mental work qualities. On the other hand, an alternative scenario is conceivable where the new production model becomes a synonym for "software from the assembly line" and for new forms of control over "exchangeable" IT work.

Looking at these two opposed scenarios, companies and the IT community currently face important decisions. For the future orientation of the new production model, which means, for the future of software development, setting the course in five crucial points will be decisive:

- real empowerment of teams versus group work at the production line,
- transparency by trust versus transparency as control,
- focus on innovation and creativity versus "execution" of the backlog,
- sustainable work pace in software development versus work under permanent time pressure,
- systematic use and cultivation of "slack" versus one-dimensional orientation on elimination of "waste".

References

Agile Manifesto (2001) Manifesto for Agile software development. http://agilemanifesto.org/. Accessed 13 Feb 2013
Antonovsky A (1979) Health, stress and coping. In: New perspectives on mental and physical well-being. Jossey-Bass, San Francisco
Boes A (2004) Offshoring in der IT-Industrie. Strategien der Internationalisierung und Auslagerung im Bereich Software und IT-Dienstleistungen. In: Boes A, Schwemmle M (eds) Herausforderung Offshoring: Internationalisierung und Auslagerung von IT-Dienstleistungen. Edition der Hans-Böckler-Stiftung, Düsseldorf, pp 9–140
Boes A, Kämpf T (2006) Offshoring und die Notwendigkeit nachhaltiger Internationalisierungsstrategien. Informatik Spektrum: Organ der Gesellschaft für Informatik e.V 29(4):274–280
Boes A, Kämpf T (2012) Informatisierung als Produktivkraft: Der informatisierte Produktionsmodus als Basis einer neuen Phase des Kapitalismus. In: Dörre K, Sauer D, Wittke V (eds)

Kapitalismustheorie und Arbeit. Neue Ansätze soziologischer Kritik. Campus, Frankfurt am Main, New York, pp 316–335

Boes A, Kuntz-Mayr C (2009) DIWA-IT@SAP: Agilität und Gesundheitsförderung. Erfahrungen eines Praxisprojekts. In: Presentation June 24th, 2009, at the Karlsruher Entwicklertag

Boes A, Kämpf T, Gül K (2011a). Auf dem Weg zu einer nachhaltigen Gesundheitsförderung in der IT-Industrie. In: Gerlmaier A, Latniak E (eds) Burnout in der IT-Branche. Ursachen und betriebliche Prävention. Asanger Verlag, Kröning, pp 251–268

Boes A, Bultemeier A, Kämpf T, Trinczek R (eds) (2011b) Strukturen und Spielregeln in modernen Unternehmen und was sie für Frauenkarrieren bedeuten (können). In: Working paper 2 of the project Frauen in Karriere. ISF München, München

Boes A, Baukrowitz A, Kämpf T, Marrs K (2012) Qualifizieren für eine global vernetzte Ökonomie. Vorreiter IT-Branche: Analysen, Erfolgsfaktoren, Best Practices. Springer Gabler, Wiesbaden

Boes A, Grund M, Sanwald C (2013) Wie agile Softwareentwicklung ein Berufsbild verändert—Das Ende des Einzelkämpfers. iX-Kompakt 11(2):2–4

Bultemeier A (2011) Neue Spielregeln in modernen Unternehmen. Wie können Frauen davon profitieren? In Boes A, Bultemeier A, Kämpf T, Trinczek R (eds) Strukturen und Spielregeln in modernen Unternehmen und was sie für Frauenkarrieren bedeuten (können). In: Working paper 2 of the project Frauen in Karriere. ISF München, München, pp 45–81

Computerwoche (2010) Agil—Keine Frage von Alt oder Modern. http://www.computerwoche.de/a/agile-keine-frage-von-alt-oder-modern,1231222. Accessed 13 Feb 2013

Crozier M, Friedberg E (1979) Macht und Organisation: Die Zwänge kollektiven Handelns. Athenäum, Königstein

Cyert RM, March JG (1963) A behavioral theory of the firm. Prentice-Hall, Englewood Cliffs

DeMarco T, Lister T (1987) Peopleware: productive projects and teams. Dorset House, New York

Dingsøyr T, Dybå T, Moe NB (2010) Agile software development, current research and future directions. Springer, Heidelberg

Kämpf T, Boes A, Trinhs K (2011) Gesundheit am seidenen Fadan: Eine neue BelastungsKonstellation in der IT-industrie In: Gerlmaier A, Latniak E (eds) Burnout in der IT-Branche. Ursachen und betriebliche Prävention. Asanger verlag, Kröning, pp 91–152

Middleton P, Sutton J (2005) Lean software strategies. Proven techniques for managers and developers. Productivity Press, New York

Morgan J, Liker JK (2006) The Toyota development system. Integrating people, process and technology. Productivity Press, New York

Poppendieck M, Poppendieck T (2003) Lean software development: an Agile Toolkit for software development managers. Addison-Wesley, Boston

Poppendieck M, Poppendieck T (2007) Implementing lean software development. From concept to cash. Addison Wesley, Upper Saddle River

Reinertsen DG (2009) The principles of product development flow. Second generation lean product development. Celeritas Publishing, Redondo Beach

Sutherland J, Schwaber K (2011) The scrum papers: nut, bolts, and origins of an Agile framework. http://jeffsutherland.com/ScrumPapers.pdf. Accessed 13 Feb 2013

Westkämper E, Sihn W (2010) Lean Office 2010. Erfolgsfaktoren der Lean-Implementierung in indirekten Unternehmensbereichen. Fraunhofer Verlag, Stuttgart

Womack JP, Jones DT, Roos D (1991) The machine that changed the world. The story of lean production. Harper Perennial, New York

Woodward E, Surdek S, Ganis M (2010) A practical guide to distributed scrum. IBM Press, München

Agile Software Development: What is Left to Do?

Joachim Schnitter and Julius Geppert

Abstract Agile software development is about to become mainstream in the software industry. Its introduction requires a significant change of the mindset towards openness, honesty, and flexibility. Therefore, the adoption of agile development by the industry is also a process of cultural change that takes a long time and surfaces many issues which have been neglected or hidden with other development models. Adoption of agile practices in global companies raises consequences which are seldom anticipated. According to our observations large-scale agile software development demands a management style focusing on constant learning and communication, a certain degree of up-front planning to support agility and emergent design, and in-depth examination of software development practices that should not only be seen as rituals of predefined process models. They should rather be regarded as tools in a toolbox which all can be useful in all development phases. Also necessary is a legal framework for contracts that support agile software development.

1 Introduction

Agile software development (Beck et al. 2001) was invented in the 1990s by software development practitioners who based their ideas on earlier process models, e.g. Boehm's spiral model (1988), and observations by Takeuchi and Nonaka (1986). Agile software development is essentially an approach to risk

J. Schnitter (✉)
SAP AG, Dietmar-Hopp-Allee 16, 69190 Walldorf, Germany
e-mail: j.schnitter@sap.com

J. Geppert
Software AG, Uhlandstraße 12, 64297 Darmstadt, Germany
e-mail: julius.geppert@softwareag.com

G. Brunetti et al. (eds.), *Future Business Software*,
Progress in IS, DOI: 10.1007/978-3-319-04144-5_8,
© Springer International Publishing Switzerland 2014

93

management. The many risks of software development are actively managed by intense communication, taking only small planning steps, and avoiding all formalism that might create a feeling of safety. Often the latter aspect is reduced to: "Only code, no documentation." While this statement is a misconception, it has contributed to the wide adoption of agile development practices because of its appeal to programmers. Furthermore, not only formal documents are reduced in number, but also reporting is much closer to reality as it exposes risks earlier. This harms the feeling of safety of managers, especially in organizational environments governed by "traffic light thinking" where it is common to report "green" project status as long as a foreseeable project failure can be hidden.

Agile software development covers many aspects of the daily work of developers, but there are areas left that are not covered at all. Although the inventors of agile development never promised unambiguous improvements, many new adopters still expect that everything will get better, at least a little.

At our employing companies SAP AG and Software AG we could observe that while many problems could not be solved by agile development, they at least became visible and approachable for the first time. So, agile development might not solve all known problems of software development but at least displays the areas where further action is necessary. An important finding is that agile development clearly shows areas where learning and education are needed in order to improve results. As described in the article by Heymann and Kampfmann in this volume, SAP AG reacted by offering a training program on agile software engineering for developers, which helped to improve software quality significantly (Kampfmann and Heymann 2013).

2 Development is Learning

Apart from educational factors there is a deeply founded relationship between development and learning. The verb *to develop* stems from the French verb *développer* which can be traced back to the Latin word *velum* meaning cloth or sail. The verb basically means *to unwrap* or *to unveil* (veil ≡ velum) something that is hidden. What is hidden are the details of the product to be developed. The purpose of development is to find out what and how exactly the product shall be and how it shall be produced later. In software development, which lacks a subsequent production process, the product is but its precise description: "The code is the truth." (O'Brien and Booch 2009). It is important to note that even the software is not what is actually desired by customers and users. What they look for is a running system consisting of hardware whose behavior is described and controlled by the software. Therefore, one might conclude that the actual production process consists of installing and launching the software on a particular machine. But the delivered software is just another (maybe the ultimate) product specification.

A different way to say *unwrap* or *unveil* is to use the word *discover*, which clearly shows that both the verbs *to develop* and *to discover* refer to the process of unhiding an object to metaphorically describe development and research. In the German language a similar relationship among words exists: *Entwickeln* (to develop) is derived from the verb *wickeln* (to wrap), and *entdecken* (to discover) is derived from the verb *decken* (to cover).

What does it mean that the product details are unknown? It means that neither the result of development is known beforehand nor is the way known how to achieve this result. A development project starts with a rough description of the desired attributes of the future product. Then follows a period of searching for solutions and assembling them. The project is successful, if a product has been found and described in sufficient detail, sometimes including a prototype. In other words, the purpose of product development is to learn what and how exactly the product shall be.

Software development is a learning process that covers three areas:

The goal. What is needed and how to construct it. In software development this includes the elicitation and analysis of requirements, the design of a suitable solution, implementation (programming, linking, packaging), validation, and testing.

The road. Procedures to reach the goal. This includes learning and selecting methods, practices, and procedures to elicit and analyze requirements, design and implement the software, validate all prerequisites, and test the resulting product.

The conditions. Environment, resources, and constraints that apply. This area is about the organizational setup of the development project, contact persons, available experts, budget, timeframe, availability of systems and test beds, contracts, rules and restrictions.

According to our observations, business management is seldom prepared for managing an organization with a strong focus on learning. Managing a software development organization according to business administration standards just does not fit. One might conclude that this statement is nothing but a re-iteration of the classical cultural dichotomy between engineers and business managers [cf. (Tütek and Ay 2000)]. After all, business administration is focused on assessing and valuating everything. Almost always business decisions are taken only after having examined the numbers. In the software industry, many valuable assets, e.g. knowledge, skills, requirements, and software components, are hard to valuate and subject to permanent change. Therefore business decisions in this industry are extremely difficult to take solely based on numbers. We believe that the classical dichotomy mentioned above is essentially not a cultural one. The cultural difference between engineers and businessmen only disguises the fact that many business managers in the software industry lack deeper understanding of software development which is the fundamental process in this industry value chain. We learned from private communications that this problem is not limited to software but might exist for any product development.

We strongly believe that education for business managers is necessary to bridge this gap in order to optimize software companies with respect to product quality, development efficiency, and product innovation. Education programs should cover the following areas:

- The dominance of learning as the basic process of product and software development.
- Innovation management which provides the foundation of market analysis, product development operation, and risk management.
- Software development language. Software development bears some resemblance with the humanities, in particular the difficulty to define exact, understandable terms for artifacts only existing in the minds of people, the difficulty to measure progress, the amount of communication necessary, and the amount of arguing that happens.
- A set of useful metaphors to translate development activities to the business administration culture and vice versa. (We wish to stress that this is a dangerous request. The comparison of software development with production processes, which once seemed to be such a useful metaphor, has caused a lot of confusion and wrong decisions in the software industry.)
- A set of useful key figures to assess project progress and results.

3 Scrum Project Management Gaps and Deficiencies

Of all agile development practices that address more than individual software developers, scrum project management (Pichler 2007; Schwaber 2004) was the first method to gain broader adoption. Indeed it raised enough attention to be included into extreme programming (XP) around 2005. On conferences in 2007 and 2008, one of the authors could observe hostile debates between proponents and opponents of scrum. In 2009 hostility was mainly replaced by curiosity. Today scrum is mainstream, and proponents start asking if some practices from pre-agile times should gain more attention in agile development. The reason is that scrum and XP practices do not cover all organizational problem areas of software development. With software development becoming an important industry either for its own sake or as a supply industry, questions how to implement scrum, measure its benefits, or scale up agility to the demands of large companies are becoming more and more important.

There is little to no information available when to apply scrum and when not. Janes and Succi (2012) attribute this to the fact that agile development practices were invented and published by reputable experts—gurus—who only sketched the outlines of their ideas but did not add details and limitations, information they certainly had but used to sell as consultancy.

Obvious limitations to scrum exist with respect to scalability. Little information is available about the usefulness of scrum depending on project type, software characteristics, and technologies. Questions on how to include experts that are only needed for a short time remain unanswered. Let us look at these aspects in more detail.

3.1 Scalability

Scrum was invented with small projects in mind, which could be handled by single teams of not more than about 10 persons, i.e. projects with no organizational hierarchy. If one adds another level of management, it is difficult to keep the same degree of agility. Information flow is delayed, and information is distorted. Corrective actions take additional time. Often conflicts occur.

The situation gets worse if teams are dependent on other teams' results. A team providing software components to be used by other teams can be fast and agile; still the consuming teams have to wait and must work constantly with the first team to keep their requirements at sufficiently high priority. Agile proponents have suggested leaving it to the teams to manage dependencies and priorities. We could never observe that this approach lead to anything but confusion.

Let us assume that to finish a given project in reasonable time about 20 developers are necessary. This number is too big for a single team because communication and conflict handling among the team members will take up an enormous amount of time. We have to strive for strategies to minimize both communication and conflicts. A proven approach is to split the big team into smaller ones, each requiring less communication. But into how many teams shall the big one be split? This answer cannot reasonably be answered without some up-front planning of system structure, components, interfaces, team skills, and division of labor. A simple split will not do much good if the expertise for certain technologies and practices is distributed to the teams such that conflicts arise as to who shall do what.

Imagine for a minute that all 20 developers can sit together to organize their work. What would they do? They would probably start by creating an inventory of skills and competencies to be able to assign certain tasks to the respective experts and to locate knowledge gaps to be filled. The next step might be to create a catalog of requirements—a product backlog—to derive tasks and activities from. At this point in time questions about the system structure will occur, because, according to Conway's law, the system structure is closely correlated with the organizational structure (Conway 1968). Therefore the team will design a system structure, or architecture, be it only for the sake of division of labor. They will learn very soon that 20 people are too many to efficiently devise a consistent system architecture. More likely 2–5 developers are required. The others will idle—or not, as described by DeMarco (1997): They would rather program something that they later refuse to discard, even if it does not fit into the overall picture.

This thought experiment tells us that up-front architecture work is not an old-fashioned practice of software engineering that is dispensable when agile methods are used. It is rather a prerequisite for larger-scale agility, because it is the only known way to divide labor, fully utilize expertise, and minimize conflicts at the same time. We do not say that this is easy. Instead we regard the architecture work as a complex planning and design activity. No matter how difficult it is, it is worthwhile. It helps getting started easily, it takes fewer resources during the planning phase, and it forms the basis for conflict and risk management among the teams.

Agile gurus have failed to write about this obvious fact. Leffingwell (2011), for example, has suggested a so-called "architectural runway" covering planning and design activities to occur along with implementation. Leffingwell recognizes the importance of system structure but keeps quiet about the work to define it. The architectural runway cannot work incrementally because it would force the whole development organization to undergo permanent change. Team composition would be ephemeral, and conflicts can be expected. Leffingwell's practice is in stark contrast to strong empirical evidence of Conway's law (Aranda et al. 2008; McCormack et al. 2012).

We regard the agilists' attitude of hostility to up-front planning and documentation merely as a selling proposition. Coders wish to code right away, and often software project managers fail to deliver a consistent plan which can be executed without significant modification. The proposal of a methodology which avoids risky or unpopular activities is very attractive. But documentation and planning are unavoidable, a fact that is not taught in the gurus' books. To say this loudly and in public takes a strong stand—and the risk of spoiling agile consultancy business.

3.2 Project Types

Project management depends on inherent limitations imposed by the project goal. One of the most important limitations that exist in software development projects is given by the existing software to be used or reused. The more software has to be reused, the less freedom the development team has when designing the solution. We wish to distinguish three major types of projects:

From-scratch software development. In projects of this type developers are asked to design a completely new solution to a given problem. They use building blocks like runtime libraries or frameworks, but a considerable amount of the program code is new. Although there is much freedom to select modules and technologies, it is expected that the solution is state-of-the art with respect to UI, technologies, security, performance, and standards.

Extending an existing solution. This development is common when existing software undergoes a new release that typically extends the previous version by more functionality, interfaces, or support for other platforms. As most parts of the existing solution are to be reused, the expectation of up-to-dateness is relaxed.

Renewal of an existing solution. In this project type parts of an existing system are to be replaced by more modern or better fitting modules and components. Sometimes this also happens during development for a new software release. Up-to-dateness of the new software parts is essential.

The three project types can occur at the same time within a large multi-team project, e.g. when existing software undergoes a major functional release. If we look at single sub-project teams, blends of these project types are unlikely. Scrum is not equally suited for these three project types. If we look at a concrete solution that gets created in one project and later extended or reconstructed in further projects, the initial project takes the highest effort. Therefore it is likely that the creation of the solution cannot be handled by a single development team of no more than 10 developers. This means we have to accept scaling issues. When this solution gets into maintenance, projects of the two latter types occur. These would benefit significantly from a well designed product architecture and technical documentation. Both requirements are difficult to fulfill in scrum projects.

According to scrum textbooks and the advice of agile gurus, software architecture is not a prerequisite for implementation but rather a by-product of agile development. We doubt that this approach can be taken seriously. One reason is that an emerging architecture is less suited to support later product maintenance, because maintainability is something which is hard to specify in a product backlog. It is even harder to test whether product maintainability is sufficient.

3.3 Product Types

The above considerations touched another white spot of scrum only briefly. It is the question whether all types of software can be handled with equal benefit using it. So let us ask some example questions:

- Can the development of a modern operating system be organized completely in scrum?
- Which practices of scrum can be kept, and which have to be modified or neglected, if complete, detailed requirements documentation and the respective test cases exist?
- Would development of a framework like e.g. the Java Swing UI library benefit from Scrum?

Neither Linux nor Microsoft Windows 7 were developed using Scrum. Both follow a mixture of component and feature project hierarchy which developed over time for Linux and was carefully planned for Windows 7 (Nagappan et al. 2008). Linux has always been extensively documented, mostly by books from the development community and text files that are distributed with the kernel code. Windows is a commercial product with corporate support for many years. Long-term support requires a lot of technical and user documentation to keep support costs reasonably low. For details about the problems with technical writers in scrum projects see the following chapter. Testing of both Linux and Windows is extensive, by both developers and early adopters. They cannot be included as stakeholders into scrum because of the variety of functions. Obviously there are better ways to develop operating systems than with scrum.

The more a software system is designed towards user interaction, the more difficult it is to specify its requirements with all details. On the other hand, there are systems and components designed without user interaction as a goal, e.g. embedded software. Scrum is compatible with such situations, but the benefits are less significant than in the first case. Scrum usage boils down to prioritizing requirements, defining tasks, and checking their fulfillment. Customers and stakeholders might get annoyed by the amount of communication in scrum. After all, they did provide a complete specification.

We assume that the development of a UI framework would benefit from scrum, because such frameworks tend to follow a strict component-based approach, an approach that makes delegation to several teams easy. We admit that we have no proof. Consumers of UI frameworks are developers. In order to act as stakeholders in such projects, they need many years of experience in using UI frameworks. As UI frameworks tend to resemble each other, the role of the product owner might be focused on prioritizing the requirements. Some adaptation of scrum seems to be necessary, but up-scaling should be easy because of the clear component structure.

3.4 Support Roles

Scrum spirit in a team can be implemented easily in the rare situation that each member can pick every task from the sprint backlog. The more specialization and singular expertise exist, the more difficult it is to keep all team members under equal workload. While this challenge can partially be overcome by permanent knowledge transfer, no viable solution exists for what we call supporting roles. Supporting roles are those which are only needed in certain situations, e.g. to set up the development infrastructure, perform manual testing, or create documentation. Even if they are needed for some tasks in every sprint, their rare involvement often does not justify to make them part of the scrum team.

A particular case is that of technical editors creating the user documentation. If the mantra of a potentially shippable product increment is taken seriously, this product increment shall also include the user documentation. User documentation usually needs some introductory chapters describing common concepts before detailed descriptions of every use case and function follow. This makes all chapters dependent on the basic concepts of the application. Changing a basic concept might require changing every chapter. To deal with this problem the following approaches exist:

- Make the technical writer part of the scrum team. He or she shall document every function delivered at the end of each sprint, so that the product increment includes user documentation. This requires that the software increment is available a few days before the end of the sprint to allow the technical writer to document the software. As the concepts of technology and user interaction become visible only step by step, the introductory chapters of the user documentation have to be rewritten in every sprint.

- Decouple the work of the scrum team and the work of the documentation team by involving the technical writer when most of the software is done. This is only an option in bigger organizations running many projects in parallel. Small organizations would have to pay the documentation experts even when their work is not required. This approach ignores the problem of the introductory chapters of the user documentation. The technical writer might ask for feedback or report product deficiencies at a point in time when the team is working on something different. Both events distract the team, and the work on the functionality to be documented turns out to be unfinished.
- Make the technical writer part of the scrum team and let him perform the manual tests, too. Many technical writers are particularly good at usability testing. As they write for the user, they understand pretty well what users expect and what they stumble about. Step by step they learn about the general concepts. This looks like the best approach but leaves two questions open: (1) How to deal with the introductory/concept chapters of the user documentation? (2) If dedicated testers exist in the scrum team, will the writers' testing interfere with their work?

None of these approaches is ideal. Fully documented functionality each sprint is only ensured using the first approach which is also the most agile one. This approach is costly by requiring permanently revising significant parts of the written documentation, and it requires careful planning of each sprint to use the full team to its capacity beyond the day when the technical writers step in. Unfortunately it is frequently unacceptable for technical writers to revise their documentation every so often. There are no automatic test tools to check the consistency of their documents.

At this point it becomes clear that agility does not mean cost saving. The most agile approach is the most costly one because it creates sort of waste in the form of frequently outdated documentation and idle time for developers. Agile development was invented to improve software quality. The budget needed was freed by avoiding complex change management, useless formalisms, and development of unwanted functions. It was never intended to save costs in the first place but to save projects.

4 Legal Circumstances

Project contracts often favor or demand a traditional procedure with in-depth upfront planning and project milestones. This should not be regarded as prohibitive to using scrum. Indeed it is possible to use scrum successfully "behind a smoke screen", e.g. within the walls of the software development company, but hidden from the customer's legal staff. We could observe that customers actually appreciate to get involved and informed regularly, and scrum does not require more of them. Project milestones are no obstacles either, because the intense co-operation between the customer and the software company makes it easy to argue that the delivery plan had to be adopted according to new or changed requirements. Scrum actually makes such discussions easier because the customer is always well informed. On the other hand, projects can be found where customers leave development completely to the software company, refusing to get involved too deeply. In these cases scrum with customer involvement is impossible which means that an important cornerstone of risk management and motivation is gone.

Contracts have shown to be a major obstacle for agile software development although—as described above—there are ways to circumvent them depending on the customer's willingness to get involved. While scrum and other agile methods were introduced to keep project risks low, purchasing agents and lawyers have their own strategy to deal with risks. Both try to limit risks by asking for detailed product specifications, plans, architecture, project milestones, contact persons, and regular communication, but typically completely neglect that the ordering party has to get deeply involved into the development project. Instead, they require that complex change management be in place to validate and decide about every unforeseen modification of product, project plan, or organization.

The rigid framework of such purchasing contracts is what kills agility along with its risk-minimizing potential. Traditional legal risk management does not lower project risks but increases them. Often this results in a costly legal battle between ordering party and supplier bringing all attempts to save the project to a standstill. We could observe that the risks were even augmented by the purchasing department asking for their share of savings shortly before the contract was ready to be signed.

Legal people and non-technical purchasing agents have to accept that software development includes a significant amount of learning. The assumption that the product can be defined beforehand is plain wrong. Projects failing because of unfulfilled requirements are often the fault of customers asking for the impossible—and of software companies tendering for such projects.

To leverage the full potential of agile development methods to minimize risks, a new legal framework is needed. Contracts for scrum projects should set out the scrum procedures, sprint lengths, project duration and costs, client and supplier involvement, backlog prioritization, exception handling, exit, and prolongation terms. As the scrum methodology is well defined and self-documenting, compliance with the contract terms can easily be tracked by a third party.

5 Outlook

Scrum has been hyped for a couple of years. Currently it undergoes critical revision, which leads to disappointment and disillusion. As software projects range from a couple of weeks to a couple of years, it was not to be expected that improvements to the methodology would be introduced early. Many involved in the dissemination of scrum now feel that they needed these years to understand all the implications of the new practices and how to deal with them. Scrutinizing scrum to modify it where necessary and daring to look at the wealth of older methods seems to be a reasonable plan for the future of software project management and software engineering.

We suggest that scrum shall be combined with the lean development practice of continuous improvement, not only to improve project-internal practices and tools, but also to improve a framework that is a solid base for future software development. Within the Software Cluster project SWINNG we work towards an improved process framework which takes all known software project management practices as a toolbox from which to select practices for future software development projects. Research is underway to valuate known practices with respect to their contribution to agility, software quality, time to market, and costs.

Acknowledgments We wish to thank the following people for their contributions and fruitful discussions: Michael Backhaus, Tim Dahmen, Martin Fassunge, Behnaz Gholami, Tobias Hildenbrand, Eva Holmes, Roger Kilian-Kehr, Alexander Scheer, Christoph Schmidt, and Dirk Voelz. Part of this work has been sponsored by the German Bundesministerium für Bildung und Forschung.

References

Aranda J, Easterbrook S, Wilson G (2008) Observations on conway's law in scientific computing. In: 1st workshop on socio-technical congruence (STC), at the 30th international conference on software engineering (ICSE'08), Leipzig, Germany, 10 May 2008. http://www.cs.toronto.edu/jaranda/pubs/Aranda08-STC-final.pdf

Beck K, Beedle M, van Bennekum A, Cockburn A, Cunningham W, Fowler M, Grenning J, Highsmith J, Hunt A, Jeffries R, Kern J, Marick B, Martin RC, Mellor S, Schwaber K, Sutherland J, Thomas D (2001) The agile manifesto. http://agilemanifesto.org/. Cited 12 Dec 2012

Boehm BW (1988) A spiral model of software development and enhancement. IEEE Comput 21(5):61–72. http://weblog.erenkrantz.com/jerenk/phase-ii/Boe88.pdf. Cited 12 Dec 2012

Conway ME (1968) How do committees invent? Datamation 14(4):28–31

DeMarco T (1997) The deadline: a novel about project management. Dorset House, New York

Janes AA, Succi G (2012) The dark side of agile software development. In: Proceedings of the ACM international symposium on new ideas, new paradigms, and reflections on programming and software, Onward! '12. ACM, New York, pp 215–228. doi:10.1145/2384592.2384612. http://doi.acm.org/10.1145/2384592.2384612

Kampfmann R, Heymann J (2013) SAP's road to agile software development. In: Brunetti G, Feld T, Schnitter J, Webel C, Heuser L (eds) Future business software 2012—Proceedings of the first international FBS conference, Walldorf, Germany, 25 Sep 2012. Springer, Heidelberg

Leffingwell D (2011) Agile software requirements: lean requirements practices for teams, programs, and the enterprise, 1st edn. Addison-Wesley Professional, Reading

McCormack A, Baldwin C, Rusnack J (2012) Exploring the duality between product and organizational architectures: a test of the "mirroring" hypothesis. Res Policy 41(8):1309–1324

Nagappan N, Murphy B, Basili VR (2008) The influence of organizational structure on software quality: an empirical case study. In: Schäfer W, Dwyer MB, Gruhn V (eds) ICSE. ACM, pp 521–530

O'Brien L, Booch G (2009) Grady Booch on design patterns, OOP, and coffee. http://www.informit.com/articles/article.aspx?p=1405569. Cited 12 Dec 2012

Pichler R (2007) Scrum: Agiles Projektmanagement erfolgreich einsetzen. dpunkt, Heidelberg

Schwaber K (2004) Agile project management with Scrum. Microsoft Press, Redmond

Takeuchi H, Nonaka I (1986) The new new product development game. Harvard Business Rev 64:137–146

Tütek H, Ay C (2000) Resolving conflict between marketing and engineering: a quest for effective integration. In: First international joint symposium on business administration; challenges for business administrators in the new millennium, Çanakkale Onsekiz Mart University and Silesian University Gökçeada, pp 535–546. http://www.opf.slu.cz/vvr/akce/turecko/pdf/Tutek.pdf. Cited 12 Dec 2012

Large-Scale Adoption of Lean and Agile at Software AG

Gabriele Kampfmann

Abstract The transformation from waterfall to lean and agile methodologies at Software AG started a couple of years ago. With approximately 50 agile teams in 15 locations around the world, the transition has at times been a bumpy ride and is still ongoing. The journey has helped the company to progress from unpredictable release schedules to in-time delivery, from unclear product and feature status to transparent backlog status. Features that span multiple teams and products are always challenging and this is an explicit area we have targeted for improvement. Another focus area was the development of a comprehensive "assembly line" for building and testing our complex suite of products to implement continuous integration and delivery. During the transition we have changed processes, tools, and metrics, as well as the behavior of the organization, of individual, and of team. This article will provide an overview of the changes implemented to introduce lean and agile in Software AG's webMethods division.

1 Introduction

A few years ago the webMethods R&D department at Software AG had—as most other software companies—a defined project model with upfront planning, a development phase and a testing phase at the end. We experienced problems with this process because of unreliable release schedules and an unclear product and feature status.

Gabriele Kampfmann (Software AG) with contributions from Christoph Rohland (Software AG), Jay Gauthier (Software AG) and other Software AG colleagues.

G. Kampfmann (✉)
Software AG webMethods R&D, Darmstadt, Germany
e-mail: Gabriele.Kampfmann@softwareag.com

G. Brunetti et al. (eds.), *Future Business Software*,
Progress in IS, DOI: 10.1007/978-3-319-04144-5_9,
© Springer International Publishing Switzerland 2014

This was the reason for the introduction of lean and agile. With approximately 50 agile teams in 15 locations around the world this was and still is a challenge. We introduced lean and agile processes in two major steps:

- First we concentrated on the base processes and structure to ensure that we are always being able to deliver our Software with good quality. This is described in the paragraph:

"How: **Doing things right**"

- The second step was to introduce processes to ensure that we are building the right Features. This is described in the paragraph:

"What: **Doing the right things**".

2 How: Doing Things Right

2.1 Introduction of Our So-Called "Promotion Process"

To ensure that we can always deliver the whole webMethods product suite with good quality we worked on the continuous integration of our products with the goals to

- Regularly produce fully-integrated and validated suite release candidates for possible delivery to the customer
- Create a suite-level continuous integration environment to ensure timely resolution of problems, to provide feedback for continuous improvement, and thereby to accelerate the ability to deliver increments of value as an integrated suite.

The result is our so-called "Promotion Process" with some important basic principles:

- Test bed for every phase is defined and grows continuously.
- Failures get fixed immediately.
- Tests for product and suite integration are done regularly.

An overview of the different phases of "promotion process" is illustrated in Fig. 1:

- *Daily product test*
  Every night every product is built and automatic tests are executed. The tests for a product cover the functionality of the product itself and integration tests with yesterday's version of other products.
  If all tests for a product are successful the builds of this product are "promoted" to the integration environment. If an error occurs, it needs to be fixed immediately.
- *Integration test phase*
  Every other day the integrations tests for all products in the integration environment are done.

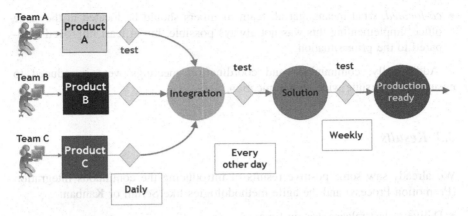

Fig. 1 The phases of the "promotion process" at software AG

Only if all tests run successfully the full set of all products in the integration environment move to the solution environment. If an error occurs, it needs to be fixed immediately.

- *Solution test phase*
  Once a week more extensive running tests are executed e.g. performance tests, tests on additional Operating Systems etc.
  Only if all tests run successfully the full set of all products in the Solution environment can move to the Production environment. If an error occurs it needs to be fixed immediately.
- *Production ready software*
  Once a month we provide a snapshot with the newest product features, which can be used by professional services, training and product managers to allow them to work with the new features or to run customer demos.

Any test failure in the promotion process is treated as a "blocker" and we have systems in place to assure attention to them, up to and including locking the source control systems.

To see the current "blockers" and the status of all products we established a daily reporting. This enables the teams and the management to take action if necessary.

2.2 Building Agile Teams

In parallel to the introduction of the promotion process the teams adopted agile methodologies like Scrum or Kanban.

To follow Scrum the teams were restructured to be

- *cross-functional*, what means that a team now includes people with development, QA and documentation knowledge, and

- *co-located*, what means that all team members should be located in the same office. Implementing this was not always possible, but at least improved compared to the prior situation.

Additionally, communities and coordination meetings were introduced to ensure a better suite wide communication.

2.3 Results

We already saw some positive results of introducing the continuous integration (Promotion Process) and the agile methodologies like Scrum or Kanban:

- Delivery: last release was on time
- Quality: Number of fixes to customers down 13 % per year
- Motivation: Result of a survey in 2011:

  - 76 % reported improved employee satisfaction.
  - Majority is convinced that Lean will bring Software AG forward in the long run.

And we see that it takes sometimes much longer than originally thought to get all the "blockers" fixed and the next promotion step done. This is definitely an area where we want to keep improving.

3 What: Doing the Right Things

When the basic processes like the Promotion Process and Agile methodologies like Scrum and Kanban were initially introduced we started to look at what we are building—which features should be implemented? The features are the things the customers pay us for.

When starting to define the Feature Management we had the challenge that we have to handle very different views to the topic:

- On the one side there are strategic requirements and a strategic planning and a budget plan coming from upper management.
- The Product Managers have the features coming from these strategic requirements, customer requests and market requirements and want to organize them as features.
- The teams want to have a single backlog from which they take their stories during sprint planning. These stories need to fit into one sprint of one team.

To be able to include the strategic planning and the budget in the Feature Management process we introduced so-called "Investment Areas".

- Each Investment Area has a defined percentage of the total investment.
- We have one backlog per Investment Area.
- Features are created and assigned to exactly one Investment Area.
- The features are ranked within their Investment Area.

To give the teams one backlog from which they can pull their stories for the next sprint we introduced a single "webMethods backlog" for the whole suite.

- Features are included in the webMethods wide backlog based on the IA percentage and their rank in the Investment Area backlog.
- Features are refined into stories.
- Stories inherit the rank of their parent feature.
- The teams take stories from the top of this backlog, depending on knowledge areas, which are currently mostly the products they know. Introducing feature teams who can work on suite wide features is still a challenge. We are experimenting with it.

The Way from Features to Stories in Sprints

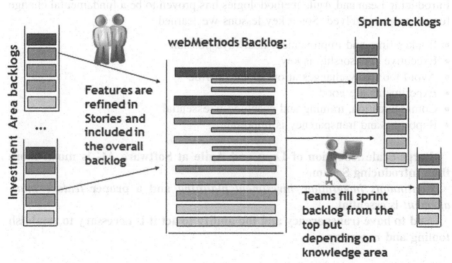

We established several tools and reports to get a transparent Investment Area, feature and backlog status.

These reports answer questions like:

- Are we investing as planned?
- Are we doing the right features?
- Can we finish the planned features in time?
- Do the teams have the right amount of work?

4 Results

We already saw some positive results of introducing the Feature Management:

- The investment per area is mostly done as planned
- The feature and backlog status is always transparent.

And we now know that we still have many areas where we need improvement:

- One area is for example that we still start too many features and therefore have too much WIP.
- Another area of improvement is that we still have "bottleneck teams". These are teams who are supposed to work on too many stories and block other teams because of that.

5 Summary

Introducing Lean and Agile methodologies has proven to be a fundamental change for all people involved. Some key lessons we learned

- It takes time and improvement is always possible
- Executive sponsorship is key
- Avoid too many changes at one point in time
- Experiments are good
- Communication, training and coaching is essential
- Reporting and transparency is important.

Large-Scale Adoption of Lean and Agile at Software AG is much more than introducing Scrum.

Continuous integration, *investment planning* and a proper *feature management* is essential.

And to have transparency and the ability to act it is necessary to establish tooling and reporting.

SAP's Road to Agile Software Development

Jürgen Heymann and Robert Kampfmann

Abstract SAP has been on the way to implement LEAN/Agile for a few years now and it has been a deep change in the organization, affecting e.g. the setup of teams (small cross-functional teams), the way they work (scrum) and also the understanding of roles and responsibilities. In this paper we want to (1) briefly explain **why we introduced AGILE and what Agile means for us**, and (2) what we have done to "**Develop People First**"—provide advanced trainings, e.g. for quality engineers, for developers, for teams, and show some key elements of those trainings and workshops. (3) At the end we will conclude with first "**Results and Learnings**" on this journey. Why this focus on 'develop people first'? Because we think that it is a key element for success on the road to agile software development.

1 Why Agile for SAP?

SAP is a large company. We are the leaders in enterprise application software, have more than 180,000 customers, more than 60,000 employees, 18,000 of which are developers, 40 years of history and hundreds of millions of lines of code in our products.

Over the years, our development processes have evolved along with the size, complexity and scope of our products. What started with 5 people and a "no process" mindset back in 1972 quickly grew into product development teams of 500 people and more in recent years. Naturally, in these large software projects it became harder and harder to build products, and overall development efficiency became more difficult to attain. For a few years we were convinced that 'more strict processes', i.e. more safeguards on all levels had to be the answer. But in 2008 we realized that this did not yield the results we were looking for.

J. Heymann (✉) · R. Kampfmann
SAP AG, Walldorf, Germany
e-mail: anna.wypior@sap.com

G. Brunetti et al. (eds.), *Future Business Software*,
Progress in IS, DOI: 10.1007/978-3-319-04144-5_10,
© Springer International Publishing Switzerland 2014

As projects grew in size the processes to manage them grew as well, but the results were not up to our expectations. Like many other large software companies we had problems with too much effort for planning, less net development time, less flexibility to change a plan that had been agreed on after long discussions. And of course it took too long to deliver the product after requirements were fixed. Thus we realized that **"more process did not help"**.

Then, in 2009 LEAN and Scrum became a serious topic at SAP. After several large pilot projects, investigations, external consulting and lots of discussions in management it was decided to change our development model from a Waterfall approach (the standard until then) to LEAN and Agile Software Development.

2 What Does LEAN and Agile Mean for SAP?

In software development circles we usually talk about Scrum or other process models that are specific to software development. 'Agility' is defined as 'the ability to react to change' and it is one of the key goals of Scrum, but there are a lot more aspects and goals in an 'agile development process'. But LEAN is more than Scrum. LEAN came out of the automotive industry (Toyota, Porsche) and is more of a philosophy of management with underlying principles and values that can and should affect almost everything in the way a company runs and improves itself.

2.1 How is LEAN Different Than Agile?

- LEAN is a broader philosophy on how to run a company and how to optimize.
- LEAN extends Agile methods to an enterprise level and is not limited to the 'development' phase. It also covers topics on roles and responsibilities (e.g. the task of management is more 'develop people' and no longer 'manage work' or 'control').
- LEAN comprises values and principles that influence the definition of processes.

As LEAN is well described in the literature we will not go into more detail here. What is important is that with LEAN there was a deeper foundation for change than just introducing a defined process like Scrum.

2.2 Scrum in Development Teams

Scrum is an implementation of LEAN principles for software development. As part of the LEAN transformation, Scrum was introduced in development teams. By now, Scrum is the new standard way to work and most units have switched over completely. This change meant in particular:

- Splitting the organization from large functional silos to small, cross-functional, self-organizing teams.
- Split work into small batches, i.e. smaller grained lists of requirements that are ranked by a product owner.
- Split development time into fixed iterations of 2 or 4 weeks (sprints) and synchronize the teams to a common 'takt' (=synchronization points) to ease internal delivery between teams.
- Break down a high level release backlog into detailed backlogs as you go.
- Perform retrospectives on all levels and in all teams to improve the work processes, tools or whatever else hinders productive development.

Put another way: Instead of a large group spending a lot of time building one large thing over a long period of time, we have many small teams building small increments in short intervals that are regularly integrated technically and reviewed by customers and/or end users.

3 Develop People First

Early in the LEAN transition we realized that we not only needed Scrum trainings and a change of work organization and roles (even though that is very helpful), but also updated engineering skills. This need first became apparent for the role of quality managers, but then extended to developers, requirements engineers, product owners and other roles. The key elements were:

3.1 Change of Quality Related Roles

Setting up cross-functional teams meant of course that the previously separate 'quality management' was now integrated into the team. And we had to change the role of 'quality manager' to 'quality engineer', i.e. from a partly administrative, policing role to a technical engineering role. Instead of old QM style of 'governance and control' we now wanted them in the team, and bring value to the team's goal of producing software. This change was a challenge for some but also a great opportunity for most QM people.

To facilitate that, we first developed a 'Quality Engineering' (QE) training that introduced state-of-the-art testing techniques to quality engineers. The training included 'how does testing change in scrum', agile testing methods such as exploratory testing, and a large segment of test design techniques (from equivalence classing to all-pairs testing). This knowledge allowed the QEs to bring significant value to the team and helped them integrate better. The course was taken by over 1,500 QEs worldwide.

3.2 Quality Workshops for Teams

Another important activity was to emphasize the notion that now the teams were responsible for quality and that there was no 'test team' between them and their first internal customers. To establish the needed mindset and technical practices we conducted Quality Workshops with every team where the team discussed their quality criteria, the agile testing quadrant, the implications of the SAP/product quality strategy for the team, and defined the Done Criteria for backlog items. The Done Criteria included things like "No static check errors", "Unit test coverage of new code >80 %", "Exploratory Test done for backlog items with UI", "No product standard violations" etc. The Done Criteria were defined bottom–up in the development teams first, and then aligned on product level. Frequently, the teams gave themselves stronger Done Criteria than the mandatory set at the product level. These Done Criteria have a very strong effect in keeping up the quality of team output. When a backlog item does not satisfy the Done Criteria, then the team does not release it.

3.3 Agile Software Engineering for Developers

On the level of individual development teams, we learned that Scrum can also create new problems and quality can actually become worse. You no longer have 3 months of 'test and stabilize' at the end of a release, and the Product Owner (PO) wants to see new features every sprint. When a team, or to be precise, every developer in the team, does not focus on the *internal quality* of the code from the start, even Scrum projects can fail. But this is not easy to achieve, as you have to change actual development practices.

In cooperation with external experts (Andrena Objects) we developed courses for developers that teach 'agile software engineering' skills to development teams. This course teaches many technical practices such as unit testing, test driven development (TDD), refactoring, test isolation, pair programming, exploratory testing, test design etc. in an integrated 5-day course. After the course, the coach stays with the team for 3 more weeks (!) to help them to solidify the practices and apply them in their own environment. More than 4,000 developers were trained so far and this is the largest training program ever done at SAP.

The feedback from developers continues to be very good. A survey showed that the work practices taught have really taken hold and we now start to see real impact in the products. The amazing result is that we not only gain significant improvements in quality, but do so without loss of development speed.

3.4 Design Thinking and Other Requirements Engineering Techniques

The next logical step to address was the area of requirements and product design. Luckily there was already a 'Design Thinking' initiative underway that had been started on a smaller scale in 2010. Design Thinking is a product design method that helps to better discover and meet the end-user requirements and market opportunities combined with a new user-experience design. Other techniques taught in this area are User Story Mapping, Effect Mapping etc. Also for Design Thinking there is now a major initiative underway to establish this technique in the development organization.

The bottom line for all these topics is: When you really want to change the quality and output of your development teams you have to change the way the work is actually done. This is all about engineering skills and less about process, governance or work organization.

4 Results and Learnings

This focus on 'engineering skills' on all levels was very well received. People love it—they want to be experts, do good work, and know state-of-the-art techniques. All training courses and workshops have received great feedback stressing that they really help 'in the real world'. 81 % of employees think LEAN and Scrum will bring the company forward. 50 % of teams have fully adopted Pair Programming and TDD. 75 % See strong improvements of quality—even at no expense to development (69 %) speed (feature output), or even at a gain of speed (29 %). However, there are of course also problems. Some developers are not convinced (yet?), some have trouble applying the techniques in their environment and in some cases it takes a while until the new way to work starts to bear fruit and deliver the speed increases that others have experienced.

And of course, there is natural resistance to any kind of change, especially when it concerns deep work habits such as 'how to write code'. Pair programming helps to sustain new technical practices as well as the fact that teams are always trained/ coached together. When a team as a whole decides to adopt e.g. unit testing, TDD or the like, then team members naturally hold each other accountable.

Also, since we are a company that is naturally focused on products, a topic like engineering methods can be pushed aside by the request for new features or the next technology. To truly establish these engineering methods as a natural way to work in daily practice means to change development culture and this requires management support, persistence and transparency of the benefits. The ultimate goal is to improve our development methods such that a changed way of working simply becomes part of our development DNA.

5 Summary

The key takeaways from this paper should be:

- LEAN and Scrum are an important foundation yet by themselves not sufficient to achieve better quality and sustainable speed in software development. In order to realize the full potential of Scrum one must also adopt agile software engineering work practices. Only then you truly get much better quality and sustainable speed.
- 'Develop People First' means to invest into all roles, enable them to perform state-of-the-art work and make improvement part of the normal work.
- Train teams together whenever possible instead of individuals. This has many side benefits for team building and helps overall acceptance and commitment to new ways to work.

Reference

Scheerer A, Schmidt CT, Heinzl A, Hildenbrand T, Voelz D (2013) Agile software engineering techniques: the missing link in large scale lean product development. In: Proceedings of the Multikonferenz software engineering 2013. Aachen, Germany

Completion and Extension Techniques for Enterprise Software Performance Engineering

Lucia Happe, Erik Burger, Max Kramer, Andreas Rentschler and Ralf Reussner

Abstract Software performance engineering supports software architects in identifying potential performance problems in software systems during the design phase. Details of the implementation and execution environment of a system are crucial for accurate performance predictions. Yet, only little information about these details is available during early stages of the software life-cycle; furthermore, model-based architectural description languages used by software architects are lacking support for performance-relevant information. Architectural models need to be extended, so they are ready to include design details as they become available when development advances. Model extensions, however, give rise to the problem of model and metamodel evolution. We report on our experiences with a variety of metamodel extension techniques, covering completions, direct invasive techniques, decorator models, and profiles in the context of model-driven performance engineering. Our goal is to enable performance engineers to find the optimal solution when metamodel variability and evolution support is required. In a case study, we extend a component-based system with thread management information, thereby illustrating the benefit of performance completions with respect to the accuracy of performance predictions.

1 Introduction

Among the expected quality properties of enterprise software systems, resource efficiency is one of the most "visible" ones. Low performance is experienced directly by the user, often leading to blocked work-flows in enterprises or lost

L. Happe (✉) · E. Burger · M. Kramer · A. Rentschler · R. Reussner
Karlsruhe Institute of Technology, Karlsruh, Germany
e-mail: lucia.kapova@kit.edu

G. Brunetti et al. (eds.), *Future Business Software*,
Progress in IS, DOI: 10.1007/978-3-319-04144-5_11,
© Springer International Publishing Switzerland 2014

revenue in e-commerce applications. The excessive use of resources leads to unnecessarily high costs, in particular when services are offered in a cloud, where used resources directly translate into monetary costs. Thus, it is desirable to minimise resource consumption and to maximise performance of enterprise systems already in the architecture design phase. In the area of model-driven software performance engineering (Balsamo et al. 2004), software architects use architectural models of the system under study and base their performance analyses on them. Transformations map the architectural models to simulation-based or analytical performance prediction models, such as queueing networks, stochastic Petri nets, or stochastic process algebras.

Model-based performance prediction, however, suffers from a *lack of detailed implementation information in architectural models*. Although this kind of information is important for accurate performance predictions, software architects omit these details in architectural models because, on the one hand, the complexity would increase the modelling effort dramatically, and, on the other hand, most of the implementation details are not known in advance. Rough knowledge of the design patterns that are to be used might already be available and can be exploited for further analysis, such as performance and reliability prediction, and for code generation.

Since the meta-models that define Architectural Description Languages (ADL) are insufficient for the modeling of performance-relevant information, they have to be extended, which rises the problem of *variability and evolution management in meta-models*. The above-mentioned problem of the need of adding detailed information is only one reason to extend the meta-model; a further reason is the need to support a wide range of technically different, yet conceptually similar middleware platforms. Such platforms evolve at different speeds, which may need to be reflected in the modelling language, i.e. the meta-model. Hence, there is a general need to evolve meta-models and to manage variability.

In this paper, we report on our experience with different techniques for the extensions of meta-models: completions, direct invasive techniques, decorator models, and profiles. From these, we discuss the technique of *completions* in greater detail, as this technique also specifically solves the problem of lacking implementation details in architectural models. As a running example, we will use a component-based system, which we will extend by task management information by using a feature model of a thread pool. This paper extends previous work (Kapova and Reussner 2010) by adding new sections on model and metamodel completion techniques. It is structured as follows: We describe the basic concepts of model-driven performance engineering and component-based modelling in Sect. 2 and introduce the common example. In Sect. 3, performance completion approaches are presented and compared. This comparison is extended to performance-independent extension approaches for metamodels in Sect. 4. Finally, Sect. 5 concludes this paper and highlights future research directions.

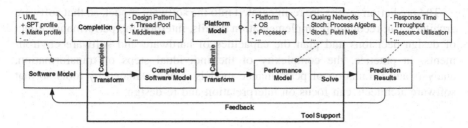

Fig. 1 Models and transformations in model-driven performance engineering [cf. (Kapova and Reussner 2010)]

2 Foundations

In the following, we present the fundamental concepts of model-driven performance engineering in general, and present the running example which will be used throughout this paper.

2.1 Model-Driven Performance Engineering

The concepts of model-driven performance engineering (Balsamo et al. 2004) are based on Software Performance Engineering (SPE) as introduced by Connie Smith (Smith 2002). SPE provides methods for early performance evaluation of software systems and detection of potential performance problems, such as bottlenecks, during the design phase of a software system. Simple models (Smith 2002) are mapped to well-established formal performance modelling techniques. These formal models are used for performance predictions, which are integrated in the software development process.

Model-Driven Performance Engineering implements this concept through the use of model-driven technologies as shown in Fig. 1: Software architects create models of a system with a domain-specific language and annotate these models with performance-relevant information, using, e.g., feature models, or UML profiles such as SPT (OMG 2005) or MARTE (OMG 2007). Alternatively, they can use ADLs specialised for performance evaluation, like the Palladio Component Model (PCM) (Becker et al. 2009). Performance-relevant implementation details, such as information on design patterns or middleware, are added to the software model. Together with a calibrated platform model that reflects the operating system and processor architecture, the completed software models are transformed to performance models. Typical modelling languages for performance models are queuing networks, stochastic Petri nets, or stochastic process algebras (Bernardo and Hillston 2007). The analysis and simulation of these models yields various performance metrics for the system under study, such as response times, throughput, and resource utilisation.

The prediction results are re-integrated into the software model, so that software architects can reconfigure implementation details, interpret the performance effect of design decisions and plan the capacities of hardware and software environments. In practice, the complexity of the individual steps of transformation, analysis and simulation of performance models is encapsulated by tools so that software architects can focus on interpretation and re-design.

2.2 Running Example

Throughout the paper we illustrate completion techniques and metamodel extension approaches based on the example of the Thread Pool design pattern (Garg and Sharapov 2002). Although architectural models for performance predictions usually lack information on the application of this design pattern, it may have an important impact on performance. Therefore, adding such information to models can improve the accuracy of performance predictions.

A thread pool makes it possible to reuse its individual worker threads for several short tasks in order to reduce the performance impact of thread management. The thread pool design pattern is usually applied if the overhead for creating a new thread is bigger than the scheduling effort for the management of a thread pool. If short tasks are executed by threads of a thread pool, this leads to a performance influence that depends on the specific configuration of the thread pool. Therefore, information on configuration parameters, such as the pool size or optimization strategies, has to be available if accurate performance models are desired.

3 Model Completion Approaches

Architectural models that accurately reflect the performance of the system under study can become very complex. Furthermore, the addition of performance-relevant details is hard to automate (Woodside et al. 2007). Woodside (2002) have proposed model refinements that add performance-relevant information to close the gap between abstract architectural models and required low-level details. These so called *performance completions* add performance influences of the infrastructure of a system to prediction models in order to increase the prediction accuracy. In the original approach, performance completions with different configurations had to be added manually to the prediction model. To overcome this limitation, automated performance completions can be realised using various techniques, of which we will present three in this section. Firstly, we explain in detail how configurable completions can be realised with higher-order transformations. Secondly, we discuss completions that are specified as first-order transformations in model transformation languages or general-purpose

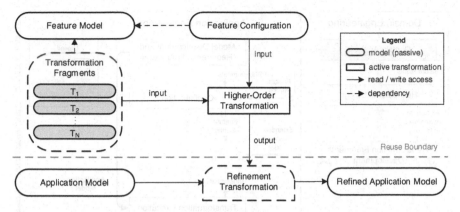

Fig. 2 Transformation process for a configurable HOT-based completion [cf. (Kapova and Reussner 2010)]

programming languages. Thirdly, we briefly describe how completions could be realised with a model weaver. Finally, we compare all different techniques for performance completions.

3.1 Completions Using Higher Order Transformations

In this section, we discuss a technique for the realization of performance completions based on higher-order transformations (HOTs). A HOT produces a refinement transformation by combining transformation fragments, which correspond to features that have been selected in a feature model to configure the completion. Once the evaluation of a HOT has generated a refinement transformation for a given configuration, it is executed on an application model in order to obtain a refined application model. The complete transformation process and the evolved models are depicted in Fig. 2.

Before we explain the individual steps of the transformation for an exemplary performance completion, we will discuss how HOT-based completions and their fragments are developed in the overall software engineering process. The model refinement process is based on Czarnecki and Eisenecker (2000) and distinguishes two phases as shown in Fig. 3. In the first phase, called *domain engineering*, reusable and reconfigurable performance completions are specified. In the second phase, called *application engineering*, the configuration and application of these completions are integrated into the steps of requirement analysis and model development.

The first tasks of the domain engineering phase is also the most important task for the development of completions: During domain analysis, possible features and configurations of refinements are extracted and analyzed. The configurability of

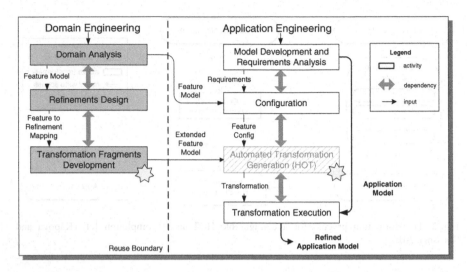

Fig. 3 Model refinement process for refinement fragments of a HOT-based completion [cf. (Kapova and Reussner 2010)]

the refinements is an important feature since it keeps the application models stable even if requirements are changed. Once the possible requirements are determined, they are used to design a feature model so that configurations can be expressed as a set of selected features of this model. In the next step, called *refinement design*, we define how features and their combinations affect the application model. Here, it is necessary to determine if dependencies between different configuration properties influence the resulting effect. The refinement design step's result is an extension of the pre-defined feature model by dependencies, together with documentation how the features map to the application model changes, called *feature effects*. Transformation fragments encode the feature effects on the model.

The extended feature model and some transformation fragments for the thread pool example are shown in Fig. 4. The example illustrates different configuration options for a *thread pool* implementation and a specific configuration using checkmarks for selected features. The example shows that features of a feature model can be marked as optional or mandatory, and can be related using exclusive or inclusive disjunction. Each feature can have additional information attached, e.g., fragments of code. The depicted feature configuration defines a simple *static* implementation of a *thread pool* with the size of 32 threads, treating all incoming tasks with the same priority.

We will now discuss how HOTs are applied to an application model in the transformation step as shown in Fig. 2. The elements of the application model that should be completed are marked with annotations. These annotations specify which elements should be refined and how this refinement should be carried out by selecting features and setting the values for attributes. This feature configuration is used as an input for the HOT that produces the corresponding refinement

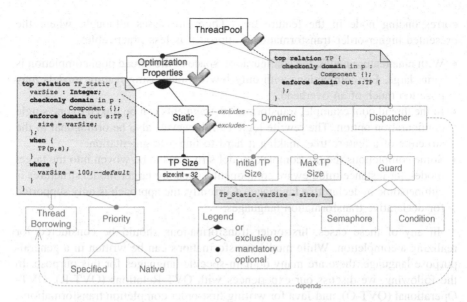

Fig. 4 Feature model and a possible configuration for the thread pool completion [from (Kapova and Reussner 2010)]

transformation. Transformation fragments, which are linked to the individual features of the feature model serve as additional input for the HOT. From these two inputs, the evaluation of a HOT generates a refinement transformation by composing the fragments that correspond to the selected features, according to predefined constraints. The HOT shown in Fig. 4 was developed based on previous work on model-driven refinement transformation development (Goldschmidt and Wachsmuth 2008) and is detailed in Kapova and Goldschmidt (2009). The resulting refinement transformation is applied to the input application model and yields a refined application model where the marked elements are completed according to the annotated configuration.

The main benefit of this completion technique based on HOTs is the automation of the completion process with customizable and reusable completion fragments. Complete completions as well as fragments corresponding to single features can be reused for multiple application models or projects and can serve as an input for the development of further completions. The feature models of a completion and the configurations for individual systems encapsulate domain-specific knowledge.

3.2 Completions Using First-Order Transformations

In the approach presented in the preceding section, declarative mapping rules are clustered into fragments, so that each fragment can be attached to a single corresponding node in the feature tree. There are cases although, where the presented higher-order transformational approach is less practicable:

- With nine feature nodes, the configuration space of the thread pool completion is quite large. For completions with only few options, using feature models may pose too much of an overhead.
- In the thread pool example, transformation fragments can be linked to one single configuration option. The rewrite logic can, however, also be orthogonal to the structure of a feature tree, making it hard to find a fragmentation.
- Some completions require complex model structures to be woven into the target model, for instance middleware components. Creating larger model structures is cumbersome in declarative languages. Currently, the approach is only supported for declarative transformation languages.

In any of these cases, first-order transformations should be considered for realizing a completion. While model transformations can be written in a general-purpose language, there are many domain-specific languages for this purpose. In the following, we discuss our experiences with QVT-Relations (QVT-R), QVT-Operational (QVT-O), and Java for writing first-order completion transformations.

QVT-R is a rule-based, declarative transformation language. As already mentioned, since QVT-R lacks support for in-place semantics, this feature has to be emulated. The Atlas Transformation Language (ATL) is a declarative language as well, but includes a *refining mode* (Tisi et al. 2010). In this mode, elements stay unchanged as long as they are not explicitly matched by a rule. Declarative languages are ideal when only few elements need to be created.

The QVT-O language is an imperative language that features in-place transformation semantics, so an input model instance is implicitly copied to the output. Actions to modify the output are specified imperatively. Further input models can be used to configure a transformation, while for simple values, language-specific configuration properties are usable. When the expressiveness of QVT-O is not enough, blackbox operations can be defined and implemented in Java. It is to be noted that, for small changes at disjoint places, an imperative transformation language requires to navigate through the model, whereas a declarative languages like QVT-R provides pattern-matching semantics.

Finally, Java can be used to specify model transformations as well. If Java is already utilized, there is no additional language to learn. Although Java is a widely-accepted, standardized language, transformation instructions in Java are by far less concise. Only basic model operations are provided by the Eclipse Modeling Framework (EMF) (Steinberg et al. 2009). Complex creation patterns can be structured using the builder pattern. We have implemented a middleware completion for connectors in Java (Happe et al. 2008), which considers performance overhead originating from remote method invocations.

3.3 Weaving Completions

Model weaving originates from Aspect-Oriented Software Development (Baniassad and Clarke 2004), but can also be used to complete ordinary models with details in a search-and-replace manner. This is particularly interesting when the same details should be added automatically based on conditions. The middleware completion for connectors that was mentioned at the end of the previous section, for example, replaces all simple connectors between two assembly contexts that are allocated on different servers to account for the performance impact of serialization processes in middleware. In such scenarios, where elements that should be completed do not have to be chosen manually, it can be more effective to use an approach that automatically completes parts that satisfy specific conditions. We are currently evaluating whether one of the model weavers that provide such an automated matching mechanism (Kramer et al. 2013) can be used to add performance details to Palladio models. This weaver is similar to declarative model transformation languages but reuses existing graphical notations. For each completion task, two model snippets are defined: A pointcut model describes the locations at which the completion should be performed by listing the corresponding model elements. An advice model specifies which elements and features shall be present at a matched location after the completion was performed. Together, the pointcut and advice model form an aspect that specifies a completion by modelling a part to be completed before and after the completion. This approach cannot be used to specify completions with complex computations, but it has the advantage that users do not need to learn a new language as they model snippets using the modelling language they are familiar with.

In order to realize our thread pool completion example with a model weaver, a pointcut model could be used to match all executions of short-running tasks that shall be executed by worker threads. A corresponding advice model could then specify the addition of a thread pool and replace a matched task execution by a call to this thread pool. Each configuration of a thread pool would require a separate pointcut model but it would not be necessary to explicitly mark tasks for the pool.

3.4 Comparison

To summarize advantages and disadvantages of the four different completion techniques we compare them in Table 1. The completion techniques based on Higher-Order Transformations (HOTs), Model Transformation Languages (MTLs), General-Purpose Programming Languages (GPPLs), and model weaving are listed in separate rows. The columns list individual properties so that each entry specifies whether a given property can be classified as an advantage (+), as a disadvantage (−) or whether no clear classification was possible (∼).

Table 1 Comparison of the advantages (+) and disadvantages (−) of completion techniques

	Configurability	Auto-matching	Accessibility	Tool-support	Expressiveness
HOTs	+	~	−	~	+
MTLs	−	~	~	+	~
GPPLs	−	−	~	+	+
Weaving	−	+	+	~	−

We present five properties which have influenced decisions on completion techniques that have been taken in the context of Palladio. A completion is configurable if the completed details vary according to a configuration. It provides automated matching if parts that should be completed are detected based on a process that does not need to explicitly specified. A completion technique is accessible if its application has few prerequisites, such as specific know-how or tooling. It provides good tool-support if its implementation is only based on mature and reliable components. The expressiveness of a completion technique is determined by the different completion scenarios that can be realized with it. Altogether, the comparison demonstrates that no completion technique is recommendable for all completion scenarios. For every technique, there is a set of advantages or an individual advantage that distinguishes it from all other techniques and for almost every combination of desired properties, there is a technique to be favoured.

4 Comparison to Other Metamodel Extension Approaches

Besides completions, there are other approaches that extend metamodels with additional information. These approaches can also be used for performance-relevant amendments to model-based architectural descriptions. In this section, we will give an overview over existing approaches, categorize them and compare the approaches with respect to the applicability to performance engineering.

4.1 Invasive Metamodel Extension

The easiest and most straight-forward way of extending a metamodel by additional information is to modify the metamodel directly, i.e., to introduce new elements and relations and modify the existing ones. We call this approach *invasive* because it requires that existing instances of the metamodels and existing transformations *co-evolve* to conform to the modified metamodels (Herrmannsdörfer et al. 2011; Kruse 2011). Modifications between different versions of a metamodel can be determined by state-based approaches, which calculate the difference (EMF-Compare (2013), EMFDiff/Merge (2013), or by delta-based approaches, which record the editing steps or allow the definition of specific refactorings (Cope/Edapt 2013; Herrmannsdöerfer et al. 2008). To estimate the impact of metamodel changes on existing instances during the process of editing the metamodel, classification schemes for metamodel evolution (Becker et al. 2007; Burger and Gruschko 2010) can be used. They provide a severity analysis and determine for atomic metamodel changes if they break the conformity of existing instances to the new version of a metamodel.

In the thread pool example of Sect. 3.1, the PCM metamodel would have to be extended by elements that describe the concept of a thread, and by design patterns that can be parameterised. Based on a change impact analysis, the metamodel engineer can evaluate the planned changes to PCM with respect to existing instances. A migration script should be provided and can be created with Edapt. The greatest manual effort would however have to be spend to adapt the existing transformations to other analysis models and to extend the simulation engines, so that the semantics of the threads is respected in the performance prediction.

If the information which is to be added in the course of a metamodel extension is already expressed by an existing metamodel, *model composition* approaches (Bézivin et al. 2006; Herrmann et al. 2007) can be used to integrate information into a new target metamodel, which has to be created beforehand. These approaches are less invasive than the co-evolution approaches mentioned above, since they do not require the modification of the original metamodels, but require the definition of a new target metamodel and sometimes glue code. Existing tooling has to be adapted to work with the new target metamodel, so we also categorize these approaches as invasive.

4.2 Decorator Models

In order to ease evolution of metamodels and their instances, metamodel extensions should be isolated from the core metamodel. When we design a completion, there are two scenarios for extending an architectural model, marking existing language concepts and adding new language concepts.

With EMF, metamodels can have references to separate metamodels. This mechanism is suitable for *mark models*, where existing architectural elements are decorated with extra information that is required by certain completion steps. The thread pool example from Sect. 3.1 uses this concept to mark elements for completion, and at the same time, to parametrize the completion via instances of a feature model.

Some completions, however, require additional concepts to be added the architectural metamodel, for example middleware concepts. In such cases, a decorating model is insufficient, because elements of the decorated model cannot refer to elements of the decorator model. Although existing classes from the architectural model can be specialized in the decorator model, they cannot be referenced from the architectural model. Hence, additional concepts can only be introduced intrusively, or by utilizing a more sophisticated approach.

4.3 Profiles

Another technique for language extension uses *stereotypes* which are organized in *profiles*. This approach is particularly popular in the context of the Unified Modelling Language (UML). Some UML profiles, such as MARTE and SysML, are widely used, supported by common UML tools and have been standardised by the Object Management Group (OMG). If a UML stereotype is applied to an element, then, values for features that are defined for the stereotype can be added to the element. Because multiple stereotypes can be applied to a single element, profiles introduce a mechanism to a modelling language that is similar to multiple inheritance.

Extension mechanisms based on stereotypes are also being developed for non-UML models. For metamodels that are developed with the Eclipse Modeling Framework (EMF), stereotypes can be defined with the EMF Profiles approach (Langer et al. 2011, 2012). This profile mechanism makes it possible to extend every modelling language that was defined using Ecore, which is the metamodelling language of EMF. Such profiles can be defined identically for different metamodels; their stereotypes can be generically applied to instances of various metamodels. Therefore, tools and editors for these stereotypes can be reused for various metamodels.

Profiles cannot be used for all types of extensions, but provide type-safety and flexibility in a non-invasive way. If existing model elements cannot be identified as unique anchor for new information, the limits of profiles are reached. In all other cases, stereotypes can be used to add type-safe information, since it can be defined which metaclasses may be extended by a stereotype. Stereotypes provide flexibility because they can add simple-typed information as well as links to information that is expressed using new metamodels. Profiles are non-invasive, because their definition and application does not interfere with models and tools of the original metamodel. Due to these advantages, we are currently integrating EMF Profiles into the Palladio Bench (Kramer et al. 2012), so that future extensions can define profiles.

In the context of the thread pool example, it would be possible to define a profile with a stereotype for marking tasks to be delegated to worker threads of a pool. Another stereotype could extend elements of the resource environment model of Palladio, so that they capture information of thread pools. Configuration options for a specific pool could be expressed with attributes of stereotypes. This way, thread pools could be used without side-effects on existing transformations and editors.

Table 2 Comparison of the advantages and disadvantages of metamodel extension technologies

	Advantages	Disadvantages
Invasive	• Full flexibility	• Breaks compatibility with existing tools
	• Central persistence of information	• Migration of existing instances and transformations necessary
Non-invasive	• Compatibility to existing tools, instances, and transformations	• Limited to structure of original metamodels
	• Modularity (small core metamodel, multiple extensions for same metamodel)	• Higher complexity for transformations
		• Co-evolution of metamodels and extensions

4.4 Comparison

In performance engineering, architecture models are often used together with transformations into other formalisms for further analysis or simulation. With non-invasive approaches, these transformations become more complex since information has to be gathered or computed from the original models plus the extensions. It is possible that an intermediate model has to be created first, which increases the number of artifacts and the size of the transformations. Architecture models may also be used without the performance information by other developers. Non-invasive approaches separate the different kinds of additional information and keep the core metamodel compact.

A general preference for invasive or non-invasive approaches cannot be given since the aptitude of an approach depends on the properties of the actual projects, such as the importance of tool and instance compatibility, the kind of extensions, and the availability of migration tools like Edapt. The decision criteria for the aforementioned approaches are displayed in Table 2.

With respect to the thread pool example, we decided for the completion approach, which can be seen as a special case of a decorator model, since the feature model extends the information of PCM non-intrusively. An invasive approach would have had the significant disadvantage of requiring large efforts to adapt existing transformations and Palladio's simulation engine. Furthermore, details on thread management are not on the same level of abstraction as the rest of the PCM, so separating these from the PCM metamodel preserves the clarity of the architectural model.

5 Conclusion

Model-based performance prediction approaches face several challenges of model and metamodel evolution and extension. Model completions, direct invasive extension techniques, decorator models, and profiles address these challenges by reducing the necessary modelling effort for software architects and performance analysts as well as the complexity of software architecture models.

In this paper, we have presented a first evaluation of existing research approaches and developer tools for metamodel extension. We have compared different approaches for model completion and reported on our experience with their application. A more detailed analysis of these approaches is part of future work. This includes an empirical study comparing developer efforts and expressive powers of the approaches when applied to performance engineering. Results presented herein could form the basis for such work.

The key challenge of performance engineering is finding the right performance abstraction for the system under study. We believe that model-driven technologies and today's MDD tools offer great possibilities for software developers, leading to more precise knowledge about performance properties of a software system, and, in the end, to software of higher quality.

References

Balsamo S et al (2004) Model-based performance prediction in software development: a survey. Trans Softw Eng 30(5):295–310

Baniassad E, Clarke S (2004) Theme: an approach for aspect-oriented analysis and design. In: Proceedings of the 26th international conference on software engineering. ICSE'04. IEEE Computer Society, Washington, DC, USA, pp 158–167

Becker S, Koziolek H, Reussner R (2007) Model-based performance prediction with the Palladio component model. In: Proceedings of the 6th international workshop on software and performance (WOSP2007). SIGSOFT software engineering notes. ACM, New York, USA, pp 56–67

Becker S, Koziolek H, Reussner R (2009) The Palladio component model for model-driven performance prediction. J Syst Softw 82:3–22

Bernardo M, Hillston J (eds) (2007) Formal methods for performance evaluation (7th international school on formal methods for the design of computer, communication, and software systems, SFM2007). Lecture notes in computer science, vol 4486. Springer, Berlin

Bézivin J et al (2006) A canonical scheme for model composition. In: Rensink A, Warmer J (eds) Model driven architecture-foundations and applications. LNCS, vol 4066. Springer, Berlin, pp 346–360

Burger E, Gruschko B (2010) A change metamodel for the evolution of MOF-based metamodels. In: Engels G, Karagiannis D, Mayr HC (eds) Modellierung 2010. GI-LNI, vol P-161. Klagenfurt

Czarnecki K, Eisenecker UW (2000) Generative programming: methods, tools and applications. Addison-Wesley, Boston

Edapt: framework for ecore model adaptation and instance migration. Retrieved 5 Apr 2013. http://www.eclipse.org/edapt/

EMF compare. Retrieved 5 Apr 2013. Dec 2013. http://wiki.eclipse.org/EMF/_Compare/FAQ

EMF diff/merge. Retrieved 5 Apr 2013. http://www.eclipse.org/diffmerge/

Garg RP, Sharapov I (2002) Techniques for optimizing applications: high performance computing. Prentice Hall Professional Technical Reference

Goldschmidt T, Wachsmuth G (2008) Refinement transformation support for QVT relational transformations. In: 3rd workshop on model driven software engineering (MDSE 2008)

Happe J et al (2008) A pattern-based performance completion for message-oriented middleware. In: Proceedings of the 7th international workshop on software and performance (WOSP'08). ACM, Princeton, USA, pp 165–176

Herrmann C et al (2007) An algebraic view on the semantics of model composition. In: Akehurst D, Vogel R, Paige R (eds) Model driven architecture—foundations and applications. Lecture notes in computer science, vol 4530. Springer, Berlin, pp 99–113

Herrmannsdoerfer M, Benz S, Juergens E (2008) COPE: a language for the coupled evolution of metamodels and models. In: Proceedings of the 1st international workshop on model co-evolution and consistency management

Herrmannsdörfer M, Vermolen SD, Wachsmuth G (2011) An extensive catalog of operators for the coupled evolution of metamodels and models. In: Proceedings of the third international conference on software language engineering. SLE'10. Springer, Berlin

Kapova L, Goldschmidt T (2009) Automated feature model-based generation of refinement transformations. In: Proceedings of the 35th EUROMICRO conference on software engineering and advanced applications (SEAA). IEEE

Kapova L, Reussner R (2010) Application of advanced model-driven techniques in performance engineering. In: Aldini A et al (ed) Computer performance engineering. Lecture notes in computer science, vol 6342. Springer, Berlin, pp 17–36 10.1007/978-3-642-15784-4_2

Kramer ME et al (2012) Extending the Palladio component model using profiles and stereotypes. In: Becker S et al (ed) Proceedings of Palladio days 2012 (appeared as technical report). Karlsruhe reports in informatics 2012, 21. KIT, Faculty of Informatics, Karlsruhe, pp 7–15

Kramer ME et al (2013) Achieving practical genericity in model weaving through extensibility. In: Duddy K, Kappel G (eds) Theory and practice of model transformations. Lecture notes in computer science, vol 7909. Springer, Berlin, pp 108–124

Kruse S (2011) On the use of operators for the co-evolution of metamodels and transformations. In: Schätz B et al (ed) International workshop on models and evolution. ACM/IEEE 14th international conference on model driven engineering languages and systems. Wellington, New Zealand

Langer P et al (2011) From UML profiles to EMF profiles and beyond. In: Bishop J, Vallecillo A (eds) Objects, models, components, patterns. Lecture notes in computer science, vol 6705. Springer, Berlin, pp 52–67

Langer P et al (2012) EMF profiles: a lightweight extension approach for EMF models. J Object Technol 8:1–29

OMG (2005) UML Profile for schedulability, performance and time. http://www.omg.org/cgi-bin/doc?formal/2005-01-02. Last Retrieved 13 Jan 2008

OMG (2007) UML profile for modeling and analysis of real-time and embedded systems (MARTE), Beta 1. Last Retrieved 13 Jan 2008

Smith CU (2002) Performance solutions: a practical guide to creating responsive, scalable software. Addison-Wesley, Boston

Steinberg D et al (2009) EMF: eclipse modeling framework 2.0, 2nd edn. Addison-Wesley Professional, Boston

Tisi M, Cabot J, Jouault F (2010) Improving higher-order transformations support in ATL. In: Proceedings of the third international conference on theory and practice of model transformations. ICMT'10. Springer, Málaga, Spain, pp 215–229

Woodside M (2002) Tutorial introduction to layered modeling of software performance. Last Retrieved 13 Jan 2008

Woodside M, Franks G, Petriu DC (2007) The future of software performance engineering. In: Proceedings of ICSE 2007, future of SE. IEEE Computer Society, Washington, DC, USA, pp 171–187

Curricula Vitae

Boes, Andreas (PD Dr.), ISF München

PD Dr. Andreas Boes is a Sociologist with many years of experience in research and consulting. He is a senior researcher and member of the board at the Institut für Sozialwissenschaftliche Forschung—ISF München. In addition he is a senior lecturer at the Technische Universität Darmstadt. His most important fields of research are the informatisation and globalisation of the economy and society and the future of work. The development of the IT sector and the work of IT professionals have been a special focus of his research for more than 20 years.

Buchmann, Johannes A. (Prof. Dr.), TU Darmstadt

Johannes A. Buchmann is Professor of Computer Science and Mathematics at the Technical University of Darmstadt, and an Associate Editor of the Journal of Cryptology. In 1985, he received a Feodor Lynen Fellowship of the Alexander von Humboldt Foundation. He has also received the most prestigious award in science in Germany, the Leibniz Award of the German Science Foundation (Deutsche Forschungsgemeinschaft).

El Bansarkhani, Rachid, TU Darmstadt

Rachid El Bansarkhani studied Business Computer Science and Mathematics at the Technical University of Darmstadt. Since October 2011 he works as a doctoral researcher in the team of Professor Buchmann in the department Cryptography and Computer Algebra.

Feld, Thomas, Scheer Group

Dipl.-Inform. Thomas Feld studied computer science at the Saarland University and joined in 1996 the Institute for Business Information Systems (IWi)—directed by Prof. A.-W. Scheer. He was in charge for research projects on virtual enterprises, electronic business and business process management. He was responsible for enterprise portal, mobile business and business-driven SOA solutions. In 2008, he took over responsibility for all research and innovation projects of IDS Scheer. By the end of 2011 he joined "Scheer Group—The Innovation Network" as vice president for research and innovation.

Brunetti et al. (eds.), *Future Business Software*,
s in IS, DOI: 10.1007/978-3-319-04144-5,
International Publishing Switzerland 2014

Fischer, Stephan (Dr.), SAP AG

Dr. Stephan Fischer is a senior vice president within SAP's strategic innovation unit.

In this role, he coordinates SAP's activities in the European research ecosystem and is the main contact for European research partners from academy and industry as well as from governments. Prior to joining SAP, he held the position of CTO and CEO respectively in two start-up companies and was assistant professor for Multimedia Networking at the Technical University of Darmstadt.

Dr. Fischer joined SAP in 2003. Since then, he held several executive positions being amongst others responsible for innovative extensions of the SAP Business Suite portfolio and strategic architecture and technology programs in the office of the CTO. Between 2009 and 2010 he was Head of product management at 1&1 Hosting, Europe's largest hosting company. Dr. Fischer holds a Ph.D. in computer science from the University of Mannheim as well as an MBA from the University of Mannheim and from ESSEC de Paris.

Geppert, Julius (Dr.), Software AG

Dr. Julius Geppert has studied mathematics and computer sciences at the University of Göttingen and at the University of Hamburg. He received his Ph.D. from the University of Hamburg in 1996. After three years as a software developer at isys software gmbh in Darmstadt he joined Software AG as a QA engineer for different products. He has also been working on the improvement of test processes. From 2004 to 2006 he held lectures on database systems at the University of Applied Sciences of Bingen. Since 2010 he contributes to the transition to lean and agile software development at Software AG R&D webMethods. He was Scrum Master for the development of a new product and is member of the ETS Scrum Master Community at Software AG.

Hauke, Sascha, TU Darmstadt

Sascha Hauke is a doctoral student and research assistant with the Smart Security and Trust area at the Telecooperation group at TU Darmstadt. He received a degree (Dipl.-Inform.) from the University of Muenster (WWU) in 2007.

Heymann, Jürgen, SAP AG

Jürgen Heymann is Chief Development Expert in the central 'Software Engineering' department at SAP where he focuses mostly on advanced trainings for developers and quality engineers. He studied Computer Science at the Technical University Braunschweig (Germany) and the Georgia Institute of Technology (USA) and got a Ph.D. in Computer Science from the Technical University Munich. After working for 5 years in development at various companies in the USA, he joined SAP in Walldorf in 1995. In the first major project he was part of the design and implementation of ABAP Objects, then architect and later development manager in the Portal product area. Since 2009 he is in the central Software Engineering group at SAP driving the Agile Software Engineering program.

Hoffmann, Michael, Scheer Management GmbH

Dipl.-Hdl. Michael Hoffmann studied economics at the Saarland University and joined in 1996 the Institute for Business Information Systems (IWi)—directed by Prof. A.-W. Scheer. He was responsible for IT Service Management and Governance-, Risk and Compliance Management (GRC) and various research projects.

In 2009, he took over responsibility for the global GRC activities of IDS Scheer and became Head of the global solution center GRC. 2011 he joined "Scheer Management GmbH" as a associate partner. Now he is responsible for research activities and product solution management of Scheer Management.

Jost, Wolfram (Dr.), Software AG

Dr. rer. nat. Wolfram Jost, born in 1962, has been a member of the Management Board of Software AG since August 2010. He is responsible for Research & Development as well as Product Management and Product Marketing.

Dr. Wolfram Jost studied business economics, majoring in economic information science and marketing, at the University of the Saarland, from October 1983 to April 1988. After graduation in 1988 he worked for the Institute of Economic Information Science (IWi) at the University of the Saarland, where his duties included supervising and holding classes, heading projects in the field of Computer Integrated Manufacturing and organizing scientific congresses.

Dr. Wolfram Jost completed his doctoral thesis at the Law and Economics Faculty at the University of the Saarland in November 1992 on the topic of "Computer-based CIM Planning—Conception and Realization of a Tool for Analyzing and Planning CIM Systems".

In 1992 Dr. Wolfram Jost joined IDS Prof. Scheer GmbH, Saarbrücken. Here he was initially the head of ARIS Product Development before taking over as the head of ARIS Product Strategy in 1998.

In 1994 he was promoted to a senior management position, a post he held until he was appointed to the Executive Board of IDS Scheer AG in 2000. He will remain a member of the IDS Scheer Board until the takeover of IDS Scheer AG by Software AG has been completed.

Dr. Wolfram Jost has written numerous articles for books and magazines and has also (co)authored more than ten specialist books.

Kampfmann, Gabriele, Software AG

Gabriele Kampfmann is Director Program Management at Software AG webMethods R&D.

After graduating in Computer Science, Gabriele joined Software AG Product Development. She worked as Software Developer and later as Product Manager and Program Manager for several products. In addition, she introduced and enhanced methods and processes used in Software AG development units.

Today she is Program Manager for a large, distributed software development unit. With her broad knowledge and experience, she is guiding the adoption of Lean and Agile practices with special focus on the feature management process.

Kampfmann, Robert, SAP AG

Robert Kampfmann is Chief Quality Expert in Technology & Innovation Platform area of SAP AG.

After studying computer science, Robert Kampfmann worked for Software AG, Darmstadt, as a software engineer. Later he held various positions in quality management. He joined SAP AG in 1997, were he was responsible for the quality assurance of SAP Business Warehouse and SAP NetWeaver and later implemented the NetWeaver Offshore Test Center in Bangalore. With his many years of experience in software development and quality engineering, he accompanied the introduction of agile methods in software engineering in the Development Organization of SAP AG.

Kirchner, Holger, SEEBURGER AG

Holger Kirchner is Director of Research at SEEBURGER AG with responsibility for coordinating all research activities. He studied computer science in Heidelberg and joined the European Networking Center at IBM in 1999. Subsequently he was a research associate at GMD/Fraunhofer Institute of Integrated Publications- and Information Systems (IPSI).

Kleeberg, Michael. SEEBURGER AG

Michael Kleeberg is working for the R&D department of SEEBRUGER AG since 1995. Since his appointment as CTO in 2002, he is responsible for the overall product strategy and definition, and for the management of global development organization. His team manages the design and delivery of all integration components and applications of SEEBURGER AG and its subsidiaries.

Reussner, Ralf (Prof. Dr.), Karlsruhe Institute of Technology (KIT)

Prof. Dr. Ralf Reussner studied Computer Science at the Faculty of Informatics at the Universität Karlsruhe from 1992 to 1997. After his dissertation about "Parameterised Contracts for Component Protocol Adaption" he worked as a Senior Research Scientist at the Distributed Systems Technology Centre (DSTC), Pty Ltd at the Monash University site at Melbourne, Australia. Since February 2006, he is leading the chair for Software-Design and -Quality (SDQ) at the Department of Computer Science at the University of Karlsruhe.

Rombach, Dieter (Prof. Dr.), Fraunhofer-Institute for Experimental Software Engineering

Prof. Dr. H. Dieter Rombach studied mathematics and computer science at the University of Karlsruhe and obtained his Ph.D. in computer science from the University of Kaiserslautern (1984). Since 1992 he has held the Software Engineering Chair in the Department of Computer Science at the University of

Kaiserslautern. In addition, he is the founding and executive director of the Fraunhofer Institute for Experimental Software Engineering (Fraunhofer IESE) in Kaiserslautern.

Schnitter, Joachim (Dr.)

Dr. Joachim Schnitter studied chemistry at the University of Siegen and received his Ph.D. from the University of Osnabrück in 1990. After three years of computer-based research in chemistry at Université Paris Sud and Technical University of Darmstadt he joined SAP AG to work in various positions in service and support, quality assurance, software development, and education. From 2000 to 2007 he was development lead and later CEO of S-Tec Datenverarbeitung GmbH, Mannheim. He returned to SAP in 2006 to introduce agile software development practices. In 2011 he joined SAP Research to conduct studies into development processes and lean development. He has been giving lectures on software engineering at the Hasso Plattner Institute and the DHBW Mannheim since 2008.

Zirpins, Christian (Dr.), SEEBURGER AG

Dr. Christian Zirpins studied computer science and business at the University of Hamburg where he also received his Ph.D. Between 2006 and 2011 he was a researcher at University College London and Karlsruhe Institute of Technology. Since 2011 he is working as Senior Researcher at SEEBURGER AG.

Printed in the United States
By Bookmasters